Making Happiness a Habit

Jeremy Kitt

DEDICATION

To the memory of my Grandfather
George F Kitt

CONTENTS

ACKNOWLEDGMENTS

I'd like to thank my editor Sarah Jones for all her help and advice and for taking the time to knock my manuscript into shape. Thank you to Sally Marshall of *Marshall's Consulting* for her help and encouragement and to Vanessa Webb of *Vanessa's Books* for her suggestions regarding design and promotion.

Foreword

If you walk into any meaningful bookshop or library there is no shortage of reading material providing insight – from academics, business and military leaders, even "celebrities" – How to be successful, How I was successful, How to be better, How to follow a completely different path...In most cases, the author is determining success – being better, being different, as a place we should aspire to. Achievement is the foundation of happiness.

You can travel all the way from Maslow's *Hierarchy of Needs,* to Norman Vincent Peals's *The Power of Positive Thinking*, through Stephen R. Covey's *The 7 Habits of Highly Effective People*, or more latterly (and scientific), Daniel Kahneman's *Thinking, Fast and Slow*, all inspiring works in their moment, pushing towards thinking and hence acting differently. Light bulb moments force us all to pause for thought – few really provide the impetus for sustained change.

Jeremy Kitt has taken a step towards a very personal and a much more specific view – Happiness as the foundation – He discusses the ever green issue of definition and context – but beyond the fleeting moment (let's call it Joy), if you can find happiness, contentment, as a sustained state in life – you will **undoubtedly** have a head start. In *Making Happiness a Habit*, Jeremy strives to show that while life and careers build around us, it is truly only ourselves who can control and influence our own happiness.

In **my** 40 years traveling through an increasingly complex, corporate, global environment, happiness – my happiness, was rarely on anyone's agenda other than my own. Sure, Sales, Client Centric, Service cultures have come and gone, however I would also suggest employee satisfaction as a standout focus, has gone with them. Once where a company may have developed a strategy that focused on growth, started with the Customer and ended with the employee, it is rare **today** to see a career path, development opportunities, a reward system running and Included under the same top to tall strategy.

These have long been replaced by a focus on self. You take control – you go find you're own development opportunities – A not so subtle change in perspective. Your career is your responsibility. Challenged by being time starved, challenged by digital, www and the **Pull rather than Push** approach to information dissemination, other than serving the Client and driving growth, most things come a distant second. We have never had more technology to help us work, decide, discover, but I would suggest the flip side is No Excuse – For not knowing, for not being informed, not on time, not on message, not on plan.

Putting personal happiness in this context and you realise it is not just interdependent on colleagues and working relationships, environment and culture, reward and recognition, management and leadership – It is a standalone – If you can create a sense of Happiness in yourself, friends, colleagues (and the workplace), that positive context creates a perspective from which to act, act quickly and collectively thrive. Of course, I should say, in most cases, the workplace, our roles and responsibilities, are something we decided upon. The pressure and culture we found – well, we knew (or could have discovered) what we were walking into. The intense focus on outcomes and results (2000's) and the behaviours that drive, well, they have upsides and as well as down – You can play and be Happy…..You may have to adjust, accommodate…

Jeremy's framework and his approach to SMILE at the very least gives you the opportunity to take some direct action and change immediately – we can all moan less, smile more and reflect on the wisdom of his Grandfather "If your face won't smile, make it". More broadly, he will leave you with a clear understanding of the physical that develop and potentially re-enforce your Happy/Unhappy state.

Making Happiness a Habit will help you understand how perspective and context frame every issue, how confrontation is the most effective antidote to uncertainty and worry. The **plethora** of quiz shows that dominate our TV these days just goes to underline – we actually love to learn. A happy self is often dependent on happy others – we need to be sensitive to the drivers that affect family, friends, colleagues. The much-maligned NHS is a great example where torrid pressure, **high** science, **and** great expectations are underpinned by what appears to be a very happy culture – a culture almost entirely focused on giving.

Making Happiness a Habit is a perfect vehicle to ask yourself, your employees, your business how can we create a better life for ourselves by being different – Being Happy.

David Fox
European Head of Sales
Financial Services
Xerox Corporation

`

1

S.M.I.L.E.

Who is this Book for?

This book is designed to help anyone who wants to lead a happier and more fulfilled life. *Making Happiness a Habit* will show you how to transform your life, so that you are more self confident, have higher self esteem and enjoy your life more.

The first step towards leading a happier life is to realise that your happiness is in your own hands. Your emotional state at any particular time is affected by three factors, your moods, your attitudes and your behaviour, and of course the moods, attitudes and behaviour of other people. All three factors are intimately connected. For example, if you are in a bad mood, your attitude towards other people is affected which in turn affects the way they behave towards you, leading to arguments and so on. The relationship between mood, attitude and behaviour is complex. To simplify matters we might say that mood is determined by chemical changes in your body, the result of hormones or drugs for example. Attitudes are the result of internal thought processes and behaviour and patterns of behaviour are result of your actions.

"Making Happiness a Habit" focuses on changing your behaviour, in order to change your attitudes and moods. Why try to change behaviour, rather than attitudes or moods? The first reason is that, it is easier to change your behaviour than to change your attitude or mood. The second reason is that changes in behaviour are concrete rather than abstract, that means that they are easier to measure. Let's take someone's attitude towards modern art, for example,. They might tell everyone that they have changed their attitude towards cubism; they used to loathe it now they appreciate it. It is very difficult to measure how much they like cubism, based upon what they say, it is far easier to judge by their actions; have they started buying books on cubism or visiting exhibitions? So "actions speak louder than words" and in this case they are 'proof of change'. 'Proof of change' is important, in the context of making happiness a habit, not because you want to prove anything to anyone else, but because you want to be able to see positive changes yourself. The third reason for trying to change behaviour is because there is evidence that changes in behaviour can lead to changes in attitude. Changes in behaviour can certainly lead to changes in our moods.

The central aim of this book is to show you a simple method you can use to change your behaviour, which will in turn change your attitudes and moods. Repetition of behaviour over time becomes habitual; the point is to create positive habits rather than negative ones.

Forming Habits

The fact that you are reading this book, shows that you are a creature of habit, you can not only read English, but the behaviour has become so habitual that it feels almost instinctual. You cannot help but read English words when you see them. You do not have to make a conscious decision to read slogans on a billboard; they come to you as if they were your own thoughts. Just as you have become habituated to reading words in English so the same is true for other habits, the ability to drive a car, ride a bicycle or play a musical instrument, for example. One might say that the definition of habitual behaviour is that it has become almost automatic; you can do it without having to think about it.

There are other aspects of your behaviour that have become habitual, in the way that you react to everyday events. Evidence for this is that it is often easy to predict how people will behave in certain circumstances. For example some people will get embarrassed if you draw attention to them, while others will always boast about their possessions etc. In everyday usage these quirks of behaviour are often seen as part of a person's personality, whereas they are just habits. You may not have consciously decided to create these habits in the same way that you consciously decided to learn how to read or drive etc. Nevertheless, these have become habitual through constant repetition.

Making Happiness a Habit seeks to show you how to consciously change aspects of your personality, by adopting positive behaviours and repeating them until they become almost automatic. In other words until they become habitual.

Habits are formed in a part of the brain called the Basal Ganglia. The Basal Ganglia are strongly interconnected with other parts of the brain including the Cerebral Cortex, responsible for thought, reasoning and memory, The Basal Ganglia are associated with a variety of functions including control of voluntary motor movements, procedural learning, emotions and routine behaviours or habits. The part of the Basal Ganglia most associated with habit is the Striatum because it coordinates aspects of cognition, including motor and action planning, decision-making, motivation, reinforcement and the perception of reward. The average human brain consists of 86 billion neurons or nerve cells. The junction between two neurons consists of a minute gap called a synapse. An impulse consisting of a small electrical charge passes across the synapse via a chemical bridge called a neurotransmitter. Every time an electrical charge is triggered, the synapses grow closer together in order to decrease the distance the impulse has to cross, thus strengthening the connection. Our thoughts are literally shaping our brains. The connections that are used most frequently help form our personality; that is our intelligence, aptitudes, and even our thoughts. There is a reason they call it a mindset. Repetition builds stronger connections in the brain that is one reason that they are habit forming. Repetition of common types of thought creates habits. Positive thoughts create positive habits and negative thoughts such as the propensity to complain, create negative habits. It becomes easy to complain because the connections are so strong you don't have to consciously think about it. The good news is that the repetition of positive thoughts is also habit forming, That is the focus of this book.

If your face won't smile, make it.

One of my Grandfather's favourite expressions was "If your face won't smile, make it". As a child, I never really thought much about it; it was just one of those things that Grandad used to say. Recently I started to wonder if there might be any evidence to support the idea. Can you actually make yourself happy by pretending to smile and more importantly can you teach yourself to be happy?

Genuine and Fake Smiles

People smile when they are happy. A smile is a signal to other people that the smiler is in a positive mood. It is an involuntary act like laughing. People generally react positively to someone who is smiling. Not so with a fake smile. The French neurologist Guillaume Duchenne identified two types of smile in the 19th century; the fake smile which only raises the corners of the mouth and the genuine smile which also raises the cheeks to form crow's feet around the eyes.

What Happens When You Smile?

When you feel happy, your body produces endorphins, neurotransmitters which signal your facial muscles to trigger a smile. The act of smiling itself stimulates your body to produce more endorphins. Endorphins originate in various parts of your body, your pituitary gland, your spinal cord and throughout other parts of your brain and nervous system. Endorphins interact with receptors in cells found in regions of your brain responsible for blocking pain and controlling emotion. There are at least 20 different types of endorphin; one type, beta-endorphin, is stronger than morphine. Smiling creates a positive feedback loop of happiness. This positive feedback loop may be the reason that even a fake smile may stimulate the production of endorphins.

Fake Smiles and Happiness

Robert Zajonc in a 1989 study[1] proposed the theory that the physiology of facial expression could be a cause of emotion. Zajonc asked his subjects to repeat vowel sounds that forced their faces into various expressions. The expressions would mimic some of the characteristics of a smile, for example, the long "e" sound, would stretch the corners of the mouth outward. Other vowel sounds were also tested, including the long "u," which forces the mouth into a pouting expression. Subjects reported feeling good after making the long "e" sound, and feeling bad after the long "u." Dr. Zajonc theorised that as certain facial muscles relax and tighten, they raise or lower the temperature of blood flowing to the brain. Changes in temperature affect the activity of brain centres that regulate emotion. In another study[2] students were divided into three groups, all

---

[1] *Zajonc, R. B.; Murphy, Sheila T.; Inglehart, Marita (1989). "Feeling and Facial Efference: Implications of the Vascular Theory of Emotion" (PDF). Psychological Review.*

[2] http://web.psych.ualberta.ca/~varn/bc/Kleinke.htm

were asked to view photographs or slides of people with either positive facial expressions (smiling) or negative facial expressions (frowning). A control group just viewed the photographs. An expression group were asked to mimic the facial expression in the photographs. An expression-mirror group were asked to match the expressions in the photographs with the aid of a mirror. All three groups had their mood measured before and after the experiment. Mood was measured by the subject's level of agreement with a series of statements reflecting their mood right now. They found that facial expressions did affect the participants' mood. Those in the control group showed little or no change in mood. Those in the group that simply tried to mimic the expressions expressed a positive change in mood after making positive facial expressions.

The greatest change in mood was in the group that used a mirror to match the expressions. Participants who matched the positive expressions experienced a positive change in mood and those that matched the negative expressions experienced a negative change in mood. Participants who were more self-conscious showed greater changes in mood following making the positive or negative expressions.

The researchers concluded that self-conscious people are more in-tune with themselves and therefore more responsive to mood-inducting experiences.

Researchers Tara Kraft and Sarah Pressman found that faking or forcing a smile reduces stress and makes you happier[3]. They asked 169 subjects to put chopsticks in their mouths to produce one of three facial expressions: a neutral expression, a "half smile" similar to a fake smile, or a "Duchenne smile" and an expression similar to a genuine smile. Subjects were then asked to do a series of stressful, multi-tasking activities. Activities included tracing a star with their non-dominant hand by looking at a reflection of the star in a mirror. The subject's heart rates and self-reported stress levels were monitored while they completed the tasks. They found that those who were instructed to smile had lower heart rate levels and less stress after the activities. The least stressed were those with the Duchenne smiles. Even those who weren't told to smile, but had their mouths forced into a smile by the chopsticks, felt more content and less stressed after the tasks than the neutral expression subjects.

It seems that a fake smile may indeed help you deceive yourself into feeling happier. No one is suggesting that simply smiling when you are unhappy will change your mood; it is more a case of

---

[3] http://pss.sagepub.com/content/23/11/1372

putting on a smile when you are in a neutral mood may make you feel better. Smiling is contagious so try to be around happy people to make each other smile. It seems that fake smiles don't fool anyone, except possibly ourselves.

Happiness as an Emotional State

Happiness is an emotional state like any other. We can make ourselves happy, just as we can make ourselves frightened or sad. When we think about emotional states we tend to think about them in terms of extremes. For example, if you think about someone who is angry, you tend to imagine someone in a rage, rather than someone who is slightly irritated. An extreme version of the emotion illustrates the point better than a mild version. Emotional states are not simply "on" or "off", they encompass a range of experience, which grows in intensity from mild to extreme. Take "happiness" for example, there is a continuum from "pleasant" to "euphoric". We use a range of different terms to express how we are feeling on the continuum, for example, cheerful, thrilled, delighted, joyful, contented, elated etc

Happiness as a State of Mind

When we describe someone as being happy we mean that they are generally happy, not that they are happy all the time. There are two reasons for this, firstly; no one can be happy all the time because unforeseen circumstances can affect your happiness. Secondly, happiness is an emotional state and being in any emotional state, continuously would be unpleasant and impossible because it would be too draining to sustain.

You do not need to be happy all the time to lead a happy life. All you need is to be generally happy, so that when unforeseen circumstances arise you are better able to cope with them. The same is true of the second statement, to be happy you do not need to be at the top end of the happiness continuum all the time; that indeed would be unpleasant.

Happiness is not just an emotional state it is also a state of mind. When we talk about someone being happy, we are talking about their general disposition. In the same way that we might talk about someone being depressed, we can talk about someone being happy. Happiness here, is not a single emotional state but the aggregate of a number of emotional states. Having lots of individual happy experiences makes you feel generally happy. To be considered happy, all that is necessary is that your baseline for happiness should start slightly higher up the continuum, than someone who is not happy

Can Happiness be Taught?

Most parents hope that their children will be happy and live happy lives. What they don't do is tell them how to achieve it. Instead happiness is seen as a by-product of other activities, for example, doing what you really love, having a family, getting a good job etc. All of these things will no doubt help contribute to your happiness. Most people spend a great deal of time and effort trying to protect themselves and their families against negative events in an attempt to promote their long term happiness. For example, you try to get a good education in order to get a job that pays well; you exercise to prevent ill health etc. These are all laudable activities, but you can do more. You can change your attitude towards happiness and see it as an end in itself. It is a mistake to believe that because you cannot control everything that happens to you, you cannot control your own long term levels of happiness. Happiness is simply an emotional state, long term happiness or contentment, is the result of many positive emotional sates and like any emotional state you can learn to control it.

You can teach yourself to be happy.

S.M.I.L.E

I have developed a simple method that anyone can use to teach themselves how to be happy. The focus is on four types of behaviour each of which is intimately connected to your happiness. The four types of behaviour are:

Stop

Moaning.

Introspection & worrying.

Learning new skills.

Empathy.

The mnemonic acronym S.M.I.L.E. is simply a convenient method of remembering the four types of behaviour associated with happiness. Each type of behaviour, 'Stop moaning', 'Introspection & worrying', 'Learning new skills' and 'Empathy' has a single rule associated with it. The SMILE approach consists of simply following the four rules to make your life happier. Each of the four behaviours and its associated rule has a chapter dedicated to it. Relevant chapters discuss the impact that each behaviour and its associated rule has on individual happiness. Evidence is provided to explain why each behaviour and its rule is so important. I offer advice and tips on how to follow each rule. You don't have to complete any questionnaires or devise lists of what makes you happy. You don't have to do any chanting or special breathing. If you want to be happy and follow the SMILE approach all you have to do is to follow the rule associated with each behaviour.

Happiness and Other People

The focus of this book is on promoting individual happiness. There are other factors which affect your individual happiness; they are external events and how you are treated by other people. There are many external, day to day factors, which can influence your happiness. However, evidence suggests that the effect of external factors on long term happiness may not be as great as you may imagine. A study[4] published back in 1978 in the 'Journal of Personality and Social Psychology' found that the overall levels of happiness of both lottery winners and people who had suffered a terrible accident that left them paraplegic or quadriplegic were not affected in the long run. According to the study people tend to have a default level of happiness and that even after life-changing events, people tend to return to that default. The point of *"Making Happiness a Habit"* is to change that default level for the better, to make you better able to cope with external events. The second important factor determining your individual happiness is the way that other people treat you. Clearly how you are treated by other people depends to a great extent upon how happy they are. How they are influenced by their own moods, attitudes and behaviour. Of course the way other people treat you and you treat other people is determined by more than the sum of every individual's level of happiness, there are social factors as well. Your individual happiness and that of other people is influenced by the culture and values of the society you live in. Happiness is subject to a wider cultural influence. We do not live our lives in a vacuum, our values and beliefs are shaped not only by other people but by the institutions in society at large. To be happy it is important to live in an environment that is consistent with your values and beliefs. How

---

[4] https://www.ncbi.nlm.nih.gov/pubmed/690806

we treat each other is largely under our own control, how we are treated by institutions is not. Institutions have their own cultural values, and for the most part, the level of happiness of their users does not appear to be high on the list of those values. In *"Making Happiness a Habit"* I take the test case of the workplace and examine the culture of the workplace and the promotion of individual happiness. The workplace is the place where most of us spend most of our time. The values and beliefs that dominate our workplaces have a profound effect upon our individual happiness. I show how a happy work culture is important, not only for the employees but for the success of the business itself. Using the SMILE approach to happiness you can change the culture of your workplace. I show you why happiness at work is important both from the employee's perspective and the management perspective.

Read this book if you want a simple technique, designed to help you transform your life for the better. Not only do I show you what to do but explain why you should do it. I present you with evidence from the latest studies so you can make up your own mind. I provide a wealth of practical advice and tips to help you achieve your aims. Remember if your face won't SMILE make it.

JEREMY KITT

2

STOP MOANING

The SMILE approach is all about changing your behaviour. There is evidence[5] that changing your behaviour can cause you to change your attitudes. This is contrary to the accepted view that you need to change people's attitudes in order to change the way they behave. (There is a fuller discussion on this point in chapter 8: Happiness in the Workplace.)

---

[5]

https://faculty.washington.edu/jdb/345/345%20Articles/Festinger%20&%20Carlsmith.pdf

The object of the SMILE approach is to change your attitude to life in order to make you happier. Happiness here simply means developing a positive attitude to life; increasing your self esteem and self confidence. The more you engage with the program the higher your level of satisfaction with your life will be. SMILE is not a set of rigid rules; it is more a general approach which everyone can interpret in their own way, according to their own temperament and individual circumstances.

SMILE sets out to change four types of behaviour, each of which has a profound impact upon your individual happiness. Each behaviour has a rule associated with it. It is not a strict rule, but a guideline. In this chapter we will discuss the first behaviour and its associated rule.

The behaviour is moaning and the associated rule is simple:

If you want to be happy, stop moaning.

Lets face it we all moan for time to time, and usually it is a completely pointless exercise. It's a strange phenomenon, you experience some mild pleasure in the act of moaning, but the effect of moaning on yourself and others is to make you more miserable. If you are someone with a reputation as a constant moaner other people may try to avoid you. Moaning irritates and depresses people. Moaning is a particular type of complaining. Let's take a look at the act of complaining in more detail.

Types of Complaint

There are situations in which we are right to complain, and some when we are just indulging ourselves. Robin Kowalski, Ph.D., a professor of psychology at Clemson University, South Carolina has identified two types of complaint:

> Instrumental complaints these tend to be goal oriented. We verbalise a problem in the hope of affecting a solution.

> Expressive complaints: these tend to be a way of getting something off your chest. We are not looking for a solution we want acknowledgement and sympathy.

Instrumental complaints are obviously valid when there is a real identifiable problem that needs a solution. What we are trying to eliminate are the some of the expressive complaints, particularly those that degenerate into grumbling for the sake of it. Complaining when there is no attempt to communicate, or solve a problem, is just complaining for its own sake.

What is Happiness?

We all assume that we know what it is to be happy and yet it is very difficult to find a satisfactory definition of exactly what happiness is. I have described happiness as both an emotional state and a state of mind. The first is a subjective emotional state which we might call joy or possibly pleasure. An example of this might be "getting a surprise gift makes me happy". The second is a general state of well-being or contentedness. An example of this might be "knowing that my family is financially secure makes me happy." The term "happiness" is actually used for two almost opposing states, joy which might be considered an active almost agitated state and contentedness which is a more docile passive state. This confusion in the meaning of the word has implications when people try to study happiness in that they are not always studying the same thing.

Why Do We Complain?

Positive reasons to complain

We indulge in expressive complaining for a number of reasons, and they are not always negative. Professor Kowalski suggests that people often complain as a way of managing other's impressions of us. You complain that you are always busy as a way of indicating how important you are.

Michael Cunningham Ph.D. a psychologist at the University of Louisville suggests an evolutionary basis to expressive complaining. Complaining is an acceptable version of the mammalian need to cry out a warning when there is a threat to the group.

Complaining is the adult version of crying, according to careers consultant Jon Gordon, author of "The No Complaining Rule: Positive Ways To Deal With Negativity At Work". Just as we cry to vent our pain, frustration and anger, so we complain to express the same emotions when crying is just not appropriate.

Yohan John, PhD in Cognitive and Neural Systems at Boston University suggests that "carrying a psychological burden can be painful, and relieving pain or irritation is a pleasurable experience. Perhaps complaining is like scratching an intellectual itch!" Complaining can be a useful tool when 'breaking the ice' at a social gathering. Complaining about the weather or the traffic has more impact and allows you to bond with a stranger, you are both united in opposition to a common irritation.

Deborah Tannen Ph.D. author of "You just don't Understand: Women and Men in conversation" believes women tend to complain in a ritualistic way as a means of bonding. This is far less common in men. Men are said to prefer instrumental complaints where there is a solution while Women prefer expressive complaints where they can express their feelings.

To sum up, expressive complaining is useful when trying to influence how we are perceived by others. It helps us vent our pain and frustrations and can help us to bond.

Negative reasons to complain

There is a more negative form of expressive complaining when the complainer gets stuck in victim mode. This is the irritating form of complaining that depresses the complainer and those forced to listen to them. The complainer has no intention of taking any advice, and is so intent on complaining that they ignore any social cues to stop. This is the type of complaining commonly known as moaning or whinging.

Palmer and Szymanska, in "Cognitive behavioural coaching: An integrative approach" outline some of the common thinking errors associated with the complainer as victim:

Jumping to conclusions. Complainers jump to a conclusion without all the relevant information.

All-or-nothing thinking. Complainers evaluate experiences on the basis of extremes. For example, "I always lose."

Blame. Complainers don't take responsibility; they tend to blame someone else or something else for the problem.

Magnification. Complainers blow things out of proportion.

Personalisation. Complainers take things personally.

Fortune-telling. Complainers always "know" how things are going to turn out.

Labelling. Complainers label or rate themselves negatively. For example, "I'm a loser" or "I'm an idiot."

Minimisation. Complainers minimise the part they play in a situation. For example, "It must have been an easy test because I got a good grade."

Low frustration tolerance. Complainers have a low ability to endure frustration or stressful situations by telling themselves, "I can't stand it."

Brain Chemistry and Happiness

Human emotions are governed by a complex interaction involving chemicals and electricity. The human brain contains an estimated 86 billion neurons. Signals are transmitted along each nerve electrically, using chemicals called neurotransmitters to pass signals between nerves. There are a number of different neurotransmitters and hormones associated with emotion. Dopamine is a neurotransmitter which has been called the "reward hormone." Dopamine is involved in motivation, drive, pleasure and addiction. Very high levels of dopamine are associated with loss of contact with reality, delusions and lack of emotion, whereas low levels are linked to addictive behaviour and risk taking. Studies[6] have shown that people with extraverted personality types tend to have higher levels of dopamine than people with introverted personalities. Dopamine is not the only chemical associated with pleasure. Endorphins act

---

[6] Depue, RA; Collins, PF (1999). "Neurobiology of the structure of personality: Dopamine, facilitation of incentive motivation, and extraversion". The Behavioral and Brain Sciences. **22** (3): 491–517; discussion 518–69.

in the brain as natural pain relievers. Endorphins are produced by the pituitary gland and the hypothalamus during strenuous physical exertion, sexual intercourse and orgasm. Another chemical 'serotonin' is crucial in inducing confidence and mental relaxation and as a precondition to sleep. Serotonin has been referred to as the "happiness hormone." Self confidence and sleep are both important in the relief of anxiety and stress. Chemicals such as Prozac do not imitate the effects of serotonin, but they do prolong the effect by increasing the available serotonin levels in the brain. Gamma amino butyric acid (GABA) is the main inhibitory neurotransmitter in the brain it decreases nerve transmission which allows neurons time to recover. Increased GABA activity in the brain relieves anxiety and reduces stress. Noradrenaline is a stress hormone closely related to adrenaline. Noradrenaline has an effect on the physical responses to emotion such as heart rate, alertness, cognition and decision making. Oxytocin sometimes called the "love hormone" is thought to be involved in human intimacy, childbirth, sexual arousal, trust, loyalty and bonding. Oxytocin appears to have different effects on the sexes. Oestrogen in females stimulates the release of oxytocin, whereas testosterone directly suppresses oxytocin. It has been suggested that the suppression of oxytocin has an evolutionary advantage. Oxytocin is strongly associated with empathy making hunting and fighting invaders more difficult. Experiments with the brains of rats and later humans in the 1960s revealed the existence of a reward centre in the brain. Stimulation of the centre known as the nucleus accumbens is associated with the release of certain pleasure inducing chemicals. The nucleus accumbens is considered to be responsible for feelings of happiness such as laughter and euphoria.[7] In fact there appears to be a chain in the biological production of happiness. The nucleus accumbens and other areas of the brain are saturated with the hormone dopamine. Dopamine

[7] Cardoso, Silvia Helena. "Hardwired for happiness." The DANA Foundation. December 15, 2006

originates in a region of the brain known as the ventral tegmental. The ventral tegmental area is stimulated by signals from the cerebral cortex. The cerebral cortex is the outer layer of the grey matter of the cerebrum. The cerebrum controls all voluntary actions in the body. The cerebral cortex is responsible for thinking, perceiving, producing and understanding language. Most information processing occurs in the cerebral cortex. Once a reward response is triggered, the prefrontal cortex is also activated. The pleasurable sensations combined with the conscious understanding (in the cerebral cortex) of the reasons that brought them about teach us to repeat the tasks that brought about these feelings

Why is Moaning Habit Forming?

Neurochemistry

In the introduction I discussed the process whereby the repetition of positive and negative thoughts can create habits. Repetition causes the gaps between neurons called synapses to grow closer together. Negative thoughts such as constant complaining, create negative habits. It becomes easy to complain because the neural connections are so strong you don't have to consciously think about it. Complaining becomes a default behaviour pattern.

Behaviourism

Positive reinforcement contributes to the formation of habitual behaviour. Think of Pavlov ringing a bell to make his dog salivate as the animal learns the association between the sound of a bell and being fed. This is known as classical conditioning. B. F. Skinner introduced the concept of operant conditioning. When a lab rat presses a certain button, he receives a food pellet as a reward, but when he presses a different button he receives a mild electric shock. Operant conditioning is the basis of behavioural psychology which examines the association between a type of behaviour and consequences of that behaviour. Habits can form as a result of a rewarding experience derived from a certain type of behaviour. Think of a compulsive gambler who started because of an early big win. According to this model, habitual complaining is the result of a positive early experience associated with the act of complaining.

Why Do People Enjoy Moaning?

Although people often appear to enjoy the act of moaning, they generally feel worse as a result. The act of moaning may be mildly pleasurable but the result of having moaned is to make you feel mildly depressed. The short term pleasurable effects of moaning are associated with production of the neurotransmitter dopamine and its effect on the striatum. We feel good when our expressive complaining has positive results, we have influenced how we are perceived by others, it has helped us vent our pain and frustrations or helped us to bond. Positive expressive complaining in the past has resulted in our bodies producing dopamine. Neurochemistry combined with positive reinforcement has built a strong association between complaining and pleasure. We continue to complain even when it is not justified as we want to experience the short term feelings of pleasure associated with complaining. That is when complaining turns into moaning. Even when we consciously know that long term we will feel worse as a result of moaning, we continue to do it as it is habit forming.

Dealing with Moaners

Common strategies that don't work

Try to cheer up the moaner

Trying to cheer up the moaner often consists of trying to demonstrate that the problem is not as bad as it seems. All this does is convince the moaner that you don't really understand how bad things really are. The response of the moaner is to complain even harder to convince everyone that things are as bad as they say they are.

Offer a solution to the problem

The moaner is not interested in solutions. Any solution you offer will either be ignored or dismissed. Typically the moaner will respond with something like "If only things were that simple." The more you try to suggest solutions, the harder they will work to convince you and themselves that these solutions are a waste of time.

Pull yourself together

This is the equivalent of telling someone who is depressed to "snap out of it." It never works and all you've done is convince them that you don't understand the problem.

Avoid them

Ignoring or avoiding a moaner makes the moaner feel rejected. The moaner responds by moaning even more to get attention. Very quickly you find you have created a vicious circle.

Agree with them

At first sight this appears to be a winning strategy, you have bonded with the moaner and recognised the perceived depth of the problem or grudge. Unfortunately you have also become a fellow moaner and legitimised their moaning. Their moaning has won you over, perhaps if they continue to moan they can win others over.

Confront them

This may work. Those who don't realise that they have become habitual moaners may stop when they become aware that is how others perceive them. There is always the risk that you will simply drive the complaints underground where you don't see them, but they will probably still be going on. This is particularly dangerous in the workplace when you are trying to create an open positive environment. Repressed moaning can be more dangerous than open complaining because it gets to stew and grow beneath the surface.

A strategy that works, sometimes

Acknowledge the complaint and sympathise

Listen to the complaint and offer your sincere sympathy with the moaner. Say something like "That sounds awful; it must be very difficult to cope with." Be careful not to sound sarcastic. Don't agree or disagree that the problem exists. The point is that the problem exists for the moaner. Avoid all of the common strategies that fail. All you are doing is acknowledging the problem and expressing concern for the moaner's discomfort, whether real or imagined. If you are lucky the moaner will be pleased that you have acknowledged them and often start to downplay the complaint themselves. "Well its not so bad really." At the very least you will not have reinforced the complaint and contributed to the vicious circle. If the moaner is a habitual moaner then this probably won't work. Habits are difficult to break and ultimately it is up to the addicted to break the habit themselves.

Complaining and the SMILE approach

Although there are legitimate reasons for complaining, you will promote your own happiness and those around you by trying to limit your complaining as much as possible. The type of complaining known as moaning or whinging serves no useful purpose and worse it can be habit forming. Once a habit is formed it can be hard to break. Ultimately the responsibility to stop moaning is your own. Use the SMILE approach to help you stop complaining. The 'SM' in the acronym SMILE stands for Stop Moaning. It is a simple reminder to stop moaning. We all find ourselves moaning from time to time, sometimes it is almost as if we were on autopilot. Simply remind yourself of the word SMILE when you find yourself griping about something and stop. In the workplace with others familiar with the SMILE method you can use the word 'smile' as a common currency, if you find someone moaning simply say "remember to smile." If they are familiar with the program, they will understand that smile in this context means stop moaning. At the very least the complainer will take time to stop and consider the legitimacy of their complaint. Hopefully the moaner will understand that it is in their best interests as well as the group's to stop moaning. SMILE is a long term approach - don't expect instant results. You are trying to change your behaviour in order to change your attitudes, which in turn will reinforce your positive behaviour.

The first step in creating the habit of positive thinking is to stop negative thinking. It is sometimes easier to stop doing something negative than to start doing something positive. Let me explain what I mean, "moaning about something" is a concrete form of behaviour. It is easy to identify and therefore to stop. The opposite of moaning might be something like "Try to have positive thoughts". This is an abstract idea and you might legitimately ask how you should do that. This is not the case with moaning. It is easy to identify and therefore easy to stop. The idea behind stopping moaning is that by eliminating negative thoughts that you will inevitably begin to replace them with positive thoughts over time. Positive thoughts will become habit forming and you will inevitably start to feel happier.

JEREMY KITT

48

3

INTROSPECTION AND WORRYING

The second form of behaviour that the SMILE approach addresses is "Introspection and worrying". "Stop Moaning" was all about changing your behaviour in order to change your thought patterns. The focus of "Stop Moaning" is external whereas the focus of "Introspection and Worrying" is internal. Learn how to use your own internal thought processes to enhance your prospects of happiness.

Introspection is all about examining your own thoughts and feelings to try to gain a better insight into those thoughts and feelings. The theory is that you should be able to use introspection to examine your own attitudes and behaviour to enable you to learn more about yourself.

Before we examine how to use introspection to promote your own happiness; a word of caution. The problem with introspection is that you have to stop having particular thoughts and feelings in order to think about them. The very process of thinking about your own internal thought processes alters those very thought processes. This problem is compounded by the fact that you are not a neutral observer of your own thoughts and feelings. It is very difficult to examine your own thoughts and emotions objectively, you are inevitably biased.

Introspection and Happiness

Although introspection may be a flawed process, you can still use it to help promote our own happiness. There are ways that self reflection and introspection can help to make you happier:

Introspection helps you to recognise negative patterns of behaviour.

Introspection allows you to stand back and look at your past behaviour and try to understand why you acted in a certain way. What were you thinking and feeling when you did certain things? Using introspection you may begin to see that you always act in the same way in certain situations. You may see that you have a problem with authority, or are intolerant in some way that you hadn't realised. Once you have recognised these negative patterns and the detrimental effect they have on your emotions and outlook you will be able to do something about them.

Introspection helps you face your fears.

Certain situations provoke fear and anxiety. You may be able to use introspection to better examine those situations that provoke unusual fear and anxiety in yourself. By examining your thoughts and feelings in these situations you may decide to either confront your fears or avoid those situations in the future.

Introspection helps to clarify what really makes you happy.

Just as introspection can help identify situations that provoke your fears, so it can also clarify those situations which make you happy. This may seem obvious, as certain things make most people happy. Introspection may help you gain a clearer understanding of why certain things give lasting happiness whereas others bring only a transient feeling of pleasure. Once you recognise the positive events in your life, you can use that understanding to set goals and plan your future.

Introspection makes you more self aware.

Practising introspection over a period of time will make you become much more self aware. The more self aware you are, the more control you will be able to exercise over your own thoughts and feelings.

Introspection helps you stop worrying about things that are out of your control.

Introspection helps you try and stand back from your situation and examine it from a neutral perspective. Although this process may be flawed it can still be valuable. You are able to see a situation differently when you can detach yourself from it. A detached attitude allows you to recognise situations where you have no control, or are unable to influence the outcome. Once you are able to recognise these situations, logically you should be able to stop worrying about them and direct your efforts to those situations which you can change. I say logically - you should be able to stop worrying, but psychologically that may be more difficult to do.

This brings me to the second rule of happiness:

Don't worry about things that you can't do anything about, if you can do something, then do it.

Easy to say extremely difficult to do! Let's try and understand why. First, let's examine what we mean by the term 'worry'.

Fear, Worry and Anxiety

Fear

Fear, anxiety and worry are all negative emotions that impact upon our happiness. They are often used interchangeably. For example, we talk about worrying or being afraid or anxious about a visit to the dentist. Although both fear and worry are negative thoughts they are different. We tend to be anxious or worry about something that we are afraid of. You might be worried about taking an exam because you are afraid of failing. You are worried about visiting the dentist because you are afraid of the pain. Fear is an unpleasant emotion caused by danger. Fear implies that you are afraid of something. Phobias, are irrational fears of things which might be abstract such as a fear of heights or fear of the dark. Fear tends to be a response to an immediate threat, or perceived threat. Once the threat has gone the fear dissipates. Worry and anxiety are somewhat different.

Happiness and the Early Philosophers

The word "happy" used to have a very different meaning. In the late 14th Century the word "happy" meant lucky or fortunate. A happy occurrence meant that events had occurred purely by chance or by "Happenchance". If you look at what some of the major western philosophers have had to say on the subject of happiness, there is a strong thread associating happiness with morality. Early philosophers from Plato to the Epicureans equate happiness with leading a good life. Plato in the "Republic" states that those who are moral are the only ones who may be truly happy. Aristotle in the "Nicomachean Ethics" states that to be happy one must be virtuous .Eudaimonia (a life well lived) is the goal of human thought and action. The Epicureans believed that our goal is to achieve a state of tranquility. To be tranquil we should be free of fear and bodily pain. To achieve tranquility we should lead a life of asceticism (self discipline) enjoy noble friendship, and avoid politics.

Worry and Anxiety

Worry and anxiety are different psychological states. Both states are associated with a general sense of concern and unease. Worry is a purely mental process whereas anxiety tends to be experienced physically.

Worry

The focus of worry tends to be negative thoughts and feelings. The thoughts and feelings associated with worry are usually verbal. Worry tends to be specific; we are worried about something in particular. Worry is not always negative. In some circumstances it can trigger problem solving. Worry is often caused by more realistic concerns than anxiety. You tend to be worried about something that might actually happen. Worry can also be easier to control that anxiety. Worry is a temporary state which is focused, and has the possibility of some form of resolution. For these reasons worry tends to be milder than anxiety. It is considered to be a normal state, whereas anxiety is not.

Worry and Grieving

Worry in the form of negative repetitive thoughts can be a means of processing unpleasant or distressing news or information. The process of working through some types of worry can be similar to the five stages of grief:

Denial. The first reaction is denial. Individuals refuse to accept the new situation. They convince themselves that nothing has changed. They cling to a false, preferable reality.

Anger. When they realise that denial doesn't work individuals begin to vent their frustations. They frequently lash out at those close to them. Expressions of anger are typically directed at the unfairness of the new reality. Examples include:"Why me? It's not fair!"; "How can this happen to me?"; "'Who is to blame?"; "How could this happen?"

Bargaining. The third stage involves trying to make the cause of the grief go away. Promising to change in some way, or do an imaginary deal in the vain hope that the cause of the grief will stop. Typical expressions of these interior negotiations include promises to live a better lifestyle, to begin worshipping God etc.

Despair. The realisation that the strategies adopted in the earlier stages of grief aren't working leads to feelings of despair. The full enormity of the new situation overwhelms the individual. Everything seems pointless in the face of the new reality.In this state, individuals often become silent, refuse visitors and spend much of the time being mournful and sullen.

Acceptance. The final stage of the grieving process is acceptance. Slowly the individual emerges from a state of despair and is able to cope with the new situation. Often individuals come to embrace their mortality or inevitable future, or that of a loved one.

Worring as a process similar to the stages of grieving is obviously an important way for individuals to learn to cope with distressing information. Like grieving it is a process that enables you to learn to accept and adapt to a new reality. Worry in this sense is obviously necessary. The process should be allowed to follow its natural course and repressing this type of worry can cause the worrier to get stuck in one of the earlier stages. Getting stuck in any of the earlier stages is not only mentally unhealthy but can also have physical consequences. Behavioural changes commonly associated with repressed worry or grief may include:

Isolation and depression. Sometimes individuals can appear very intellectual, analytic, or unemotional, they are often unable to bond.

Repressed anger. Individuals can appear cynical, sarcastic and are sometimes prone to rages. People often suffer from insomnia and are generally irritable.

Self denial. Individuals minimise the importance of everything, and suffer from low self esteem.

Addictions. Individuals' addictions can range from substances, including alcohol to addictive behaviour such a toxic relationships or overwork.

Avoidance. Certain people or events associated with the cause of grief or worry become taboo, and are avoided at all costs.

Headaches. Headaches and other chronic pain which does not apper to have a physical cause.

Nightmares.

Obesity and eating disorders.

The second rule of SMILE still applies to this form of worry. If you can change the cause of the worry or grief then you should. When you cannot change the cause of the worry or grief you should learn to accept it. You will learn to accept this type of worry by going through the five stages as outlined above.

We will consider some ways in which you might try to control other forms of worry at the end of this chapter. First, let's continue to look at the various forms of worry by considering the form of worry commonly referred to as anxiety.

The Philosophy of Happiness in the Middle Ages

For later philosophers from St.Augustine to Thomas Aquinas, happiness is related to understanding God and religious practice; although towards the end of this period there is a greater emphasis on self knowledge and intellectual pursuits. St Augustine argues in his treatises "De beata vita" and "Contra Academicos" that God is the source of all happiness. We are brought into the world by God, but have since fallen. Our souls have a dim recollection of the happiness we enjoyed when we were at one with God. Only through the love of God can we attain happiness. Boethius in "The Consolation of Philosophy" states that happiness is acquired by attaining the perfect good, and that perfect good is God. As God rules the universe through Love, it is only by praying to God and the application of Love that leads to true happiness. Al-Ghazali in "The Alchemy of Happiness", states the importance of observing the ritual requirements of Islam. Only strict observance can lead to salvation, and the avoidance of sin. The exercise of reason, a God-given ability, can be used to transform the soul from worldliness to complete devotion to God which is the ultimate happiness. Al-Ghazali, proposes four main constituents of happiness: Self-knowledge, Knowledge of God, Knowledge of this world as it really is and Knowledge of the next world as it really is. Thomas Aquinas in "Summa Theologica" argues that happiness is achieved by cultivating several intellectual and moral virtues, which enable us to understand the nature of happiness and motivate us to seek it in a reliable and consistent way. However, we will be unable to find the greatest happiness in this life, because final happiness consists in a supernatural union with God.

Anxiety

Anxiety creates a physical response expressed by such things as a palpitating heart, sweating, churning stomach, nausea etc. Anxiety is associated with both verbal thoughts and mental imagery. It is often the mental images that tend to provoke the physical response associated with anxiety. Anxiety is more vague than worry. For example you might be anxious about flying, you might have mental images of plane crashes etc, These anxious feelings arise because of a general fear of flying rather than any specific cause. Anxiety, because it is vague and unfocused does not lend itself to a simple resolution. If, for example you were worried about flying because there was a problem with one of the engines, you could simply change flights. The vague unfocused state of anxiety means that it tends to linger and is not amenable to simple solutions. Anxiety and anxiety attacks can be overwhelming and can be associated with depression and mental health issues which may require treatment. Excessive anxiety known as Generalised Anxiety Disorder (GAD) affects one in twenty people.

What causes anxiety?

When you find yourself in a stressful situation your body triggers the "fight-or-flight response". When threatened the sympathetic nervous system releases a number of hormones which prepare you to fight or flee. What actually happens is that the adrenal medulla secretes the hormones noradrenalin and adrenaline along with oestrogen, testosterone, and cortisol. The neurotransmitters dopamine and serotonin also affect how you react to stress.

The 'fight or flight' response is an involuntary response which has evolved to cope with physical danger on a daily basis. In the modern world most of the threats that people face tend to be psychological rather than physical. Psychological threats are often difficult to resolve immediately. That means that the fight or flight response remains active for much longer which is more draining, physically and emotionally. Our bodies remain in survival mode for longer periods of time. Inappropriate triggering of the fight or flight response is associated with anxiety.

Is anxiety genetic or learned?

Until the late 1990s it was generally agreed that the causes of anxiety were unlikely to be hereditary. More recent studies now suggest that in certain circumstances anxiety may have a genetic cause. A study[8] in 2008 of families who survived a massive earthquake in Armenia in 1988 found that 41% of those suffering from Post Traumatic Stress Disorder were due to genetic factors. 61% suffering from depression and 66% suffering from anxiety were attributable to genetics. A study[9] in 2009 examining insomnia in young adults found a link between insomnia, anxiety and depression which could be explained by genetic variations. Another study[10] in 2003 put forward the view that some people are more prone to anxiety and aggression than others because of a genetic abnormality. Researchers found a gene called SLC6A4 that may contribute, albeit in a small way, to anxiety in certain individuals. The SLC6A4 gene is important in the transmission of serotonin. Individuals can inherit a short or a long version of this gene from either parent. The short version transports serotonin less

[8] Goenjian, A.K. et al (2008) Heritabilities of symptoms of posttraumatic stress disorder, anxiety, and depression in earthquake exposed Armenian families. Psychiatric Genetics. 18(6):261-266, December 2008.

[9] Gehrman, P., etal (2009) *Heritability of Insomnia in adolescents: how much is just depression and anxiety?* Abstract presented on June 8, at SLEEP 2009, the 23rd Annual Meeting of the Associated Professional Sleep Societies

[10] Hendricks, T.J. etal (2003) Pet-1 ETS Gene Plays a Critical Role in 5-HT Neuron Development and Is Required for Normal Anxiety-like and Aggressive Behavior. Neuron, Volume 37, Issue 2, 233-247, 23 January 2003

efficiently than the long one. Serotonin is responsible for maintaining mood balance, and a lack of serotonin can lead to depression. People who have one or two of the short versions tend to show abnormal levels of anxiety.

Worry is a form of self torture

Worry tends to be specific whereas anxiety is more general. You tend to worry because you think that something bad will happen, or could happen to you. For example, will I make a fool of myself when speaking in public? That is a specific worry. Worrying is a process whereby you imagine different scenarios that could go wrong, so you can look for solutions to prevent them from happening. Imagining how embarrassing it would be to forget your speech prompts you to try harder to memorise it. A great deal of worry is caused by the fear of uncertainty. Often worry is an attempt to gain control over situations in which you have no control. For example, you worry about the outcome of a medical test, although there is nothing you can do influence the result. Worry can be a form of coping mechanism; it's as if by repeatedly playing over a negative scenario in our heads we can somehow magically influence it. Worrying is a form of self torture. Indeed the French term for worrying, "torturer l'espirit" translates as torture of the mind.

What do people worry about?

A survey[11] published in 'The Independent' newspaper in 2015 found that the thing that most people worried about was getting old, their savings and financial future.. A survey[12] published in 2015 by 'Nelsons', a manufacturer of natural healthcare products, found that worries about work topped the list.

The relationship between stress and physical disease

In the 1930s an Austrian-born endocrinologist working in Canada was trying to discover a new hormone. His name was Hans Selye. Selye injected lab rats with an ovarian extract. After a few months the rats developed peptic ulcers and swollen adrenal glands. Selye took this as proof that he had discovered a new hormone. To confirm his results he also injected a control group of rats with a saline

---

[11] https://www.indy100.com/article/the-20-things-people-worry-about-the-most--xJVjF0DSox

[12] http://www.hrreview.co.uk/hr-news/wellbeing-news/work-tops-list-things-brits-worry-says-new-survey/58995

solution. To his dismay Selye found that the rats in the control group were suffering from exactly the same condition. If it wasn't the injections that were causing the condition what was it? Selye concluded that it was his own incompetence as a lab technician that was the cause. Selye was an inexperienced technician and frequently dropped the rats and had to chase them around the floor with a broom in order to catch them before he could inject them. Selye had inadvertently stressed all the rats; he had failed to discover a new hormone but had demonstrated for the first time the relationship between stress and physical disease. The science of psychoneuroimmunology was born. Hans Seyle passed away in 1982, today he is regarded as "the father of the field of stress research."

How worry and anxiety affect your body.

The 'fight or flight' response releases hormones into your body as described earlier. The release of hormones increases the levels of blood sugar and triglycerides (fats) into your blood stream which are used to fuel your body when it is in survival mode. The hormone adrenaline, which is also known as epinephrine is largely responsible for the immediate reactions to a threat. Adrenaline increases your heart rate and gives you that surge of energy. Noradenaline also known as norepinephrine increases your arousal to make you more focused and more alert. Adrenaline and noradenaline have very similar effects; it is almost as if your body has a back up system in case one system is not functioning properly in an emergency. The energy giving effects of adrenaline and noradenaline are instant, while the third stress hormone, cortisol, takes longer to release.

Cortisol helps maintain your body's fluid balance and blood pressure. Cortisol regulates a number of body functions that aren't crucial when in survival mode such as the, reproductive drive, immunity, digestion and growth. The immediate effect of these three hormones on the body can include:

Inability to concentrate

Irritability

Muscle aches

Muscle tension

Nausea

Nervous energy

Rapid breathing

Shortness of breath

Sweating

Trembling and twitching

Dizziness

Dry mouth

Fast heartbeat

Fatigue

Headaches

Adrenaline is produced by the adrenal glands. Noradrenaline is produced by the adrenal glands and the brain. Adrenaline and noradrenaline tend to dissipate from your system very quickly. Cortisol is a bit more complicated. Once a threat has been recognised the part of your brain called the amygdala sends a message to another part of your brain called the hippocampus. The amygdala is associated with memory, decision-making, and emotional reactions. The hippocampus, named because it is supposed to resemble a seahorse, is responsible for the formation of new memories, and spatial awareness. The hippocampus is one of the first regions of your brain to suffer damage as a result of Alzheimer's Disease.

In the production of cortisol the hippocampus releases a hormone known as CRH. CRH causes your pituitary gland to release another hormone known as ACTH, which in turn causes the adrenal glands to produce cortisol. One of the problems with cortisol is that not only does it take longer for your body to release, but more importantly it stays in your body for longer. Stress and anxiety can cause your body to keep producing cortisol which can have a very negative effect on your health. Excess cortisol can to lead health problems such as osteoporosis, digestive problems, hormone imbalances, cancer, heart disease, and diabetes. Common signs of stress due to an elevated level of cortisol include weight gain, mood swings, poor sleep, short attention span, and memory issues.

Early Modern Philosophers and Happiness

From Montaigne onwards the emphasis becomes much more diverse ranging from the subjective nature of happiness to the cultural and biological influences on the nature of happiness. Montaigne in his "Essays" concludes that happiness is a subjective state of mind and that it differs from person to person. Montaigne states that one must be allowed a private sphere of life to realise those particular attempts at happiness without the interference of society. John Locke in "An Essay Concerning Human Understanding" coined the phrase "pursuit of happiness". Locke distinguishes between "imaginary happiness" and "true happiness." "Imaginary happiness" includes the satisfaction of desires, the pursuit of wealth and pleasure. "True happiness" is the freedom to be able to make decisions that result in the best life possible for a person, which include intellectual and moral effort.

MAKING HAPPINESS A HABIT

Jeremy Bentham in "The Principles of Morals and Legislation" outlines the utility principle. The definition of utility is the total amount of pleasure after deducting the total amount of suffering involved in any action. Happiness, is the experience of pleasure and the absence of pain. Schopenhauer, in "The World as Will and Representation " states that happiness is a wish that is satisfied, which in turn gives rise to a new wish. Suffering is the absence of satisfaction which results in an empty longing. Schopenhauer states that egotistical acts are those that are guided by self-interest, desire for pleasure or happiness, only compassion can be considered a moral act.

The Effects of Cortisol on Your Brain

Cortisol can be a very dangerous substance. It is a steroid. When used as a medication, it is known as hydrocortisone. Cortisol creates free radicals that kill brain cells. Cortisol can affect your memory and make you more emotional. Cortisol can have a detrimental effect on the creation of new brain cells. This is roughly how it works:

Cortisol creates free radicals that kill brain cells.

Cortisol is associated with the neurotransmitter glutamate. A surplus of cortisol creates a surplus of the neurotransmitter glutamate which in turn creates free radicals. Free radicals are highly volatile unattached oxygen molecules which destroy neurons. The free radicals create holes in the cell walls, causing them to die.

High levels of cortisol can make you more emotional.

Studies[13][14] have shown that long term stress can

---

[13] http://www.jneurosci.org/content/33/17/7234.abstract

[14]

http://www.nature.com/npp/journal/v33/n1/full/1301574a.html

actually alter the physiology of the brain. Prolonged exposure to cortisol increases the functional connectivity from your amygdala to your hippocampus. Cortisol can increase the size of your amygdala, by creating more activity and therefore more neural connections. Your amygdala is responsible for emotional reactions. Anxiety can induce the release of cortisol over a prolonged period, which increases the size of your amygdala making you more anxious, creating a vicious circle.

High levels of cortisol can have a detrimental effect on your memory and ability to learn.

Sandra Ackermann of the University of Basel in Switzerland, stated[15] that "Stress and cortisol strongly influence memory and are highly important modulators of learning and memory mechanisms." Ackermann gave 1,225 healthy men and women a memory test and then measured their cortisol levels via saliva samples. She found that higher cortisol levels during memory recall hindered the ability to remember.

---

[15] https://www.cogneurosociety.org/cortisol_memory/

Cortisol inhibits the creation of new brain cells.

The hippocampus is particularly vulnerable to long-term stress. Cortisol affects the hippocampus in at least three ways: firstly, by reducing the excitability of some hippocampal neurons; secondly by inhibiting the creation of new neurons and lastly by causing atrophy in other neurons. Our bodies produce a protein called 'Brain-derived neurotrophic factor' (BDNF) which is vital in the creation of new neurons. Cortisol stops the production of BDNF which means that fewer new neurons are formed.

Cortisol and the Immune System

There are two theories regarding the effects of cortisol on your immune system:

The Traditional Theory

Stress induces the release of cortisol which suppresses your immune system. The temporary suppression of your immune system while in survival mode allows pathogens to enter and grow within your body. The increase in pathogens leads to sickness.

An Alternative Theory

Sickness caused by stress is not the result of pathogens but the result of cortisol regulation. The symptoms of sickness, sore throat, headache etc are not caused by the pathogens themselves but by your body's immune systems combating the pathogens. This is known as the inflammatory response. While under stress your body constantly produces cortisol which suppresses the immune system and therefore the inflammatory response. Once the stressful stimulus has passed, your body stops producing cortisol which switches your immune system back on, triggering the inflammatory response which makes you feel sick.

In truth sickness due to stress is probably caused by a mixture of both. A threat stimulates the release of cortisol which suppresses your immune system stimulating the growth of pathogens. Once the threat passes, lower levels of cortisol allow your immune system to switch back on, triggering the inflammatory response to fight off the pathogens.

The suppression of your immune system associated with accelerated levels of cortisol is associated with other negative effects as well as sickness. Prolonged healing times, reduction in the ability to cope with vaccinations, and increased susceptibility to viral infection are all associated with heightened cortisol exposure. Symptoms of long term exposure to cortisol include impaired cognition, decreased thyroid function, and the accumulation of abdominal fat.

Other Physical Effects of Stress

Stress and heart disease

A study[16] in 2003 assessed the relationship between chronic stress and IL-6 production. The subjects were 119 men and women who were caring for a spouse with dementia and 106 men and women who were not carers. Carers were chosen because they are known to exhibit high levels of stress. The study found that people caring for spouses with Alzheimer's Disease showed a marked overproduction of IL-6. IL-6 is secreted as part of the immune response; it is normally involved in the immune response to injury. Increased levels of IL-6 are associated with a number of age-related conditions, including heart disease, osteoporosis, arthritis, Type 2 diabetes, certain cancers, and mental decline.

---

[16] Janice K. Kiecolt-Glaser et al. "Chronic stress and age-related increases in the proinflammatory cytokine IL-6," Proceedings of the National Academy of Science, Vol. 100; No. 15. July 22, 2003

Stress and healing

A study[17] published in 2005 assessed how hostile marital behaviour affected wound healing. The study included a sample of 42 healthy married couples, aged 22 to 77 years who had been married for over ten years on average.

They found that couples whose behaviour was rated as hostile toward each other had a wound-healing rate that was only 60 percent compared to the rate of couples with gentler relations. They concluded that marital discord could adversely affect the body's ability to heal wounds.

How to Stop Worrying

Everyone knows that it is really difficult to stop worrying. The harder you try to stop the worse it becomes. You become frustrated at your inability to stop worrying and blame yourself.

---

[17] Janice K. Kiecolt-Glaser et al. "Hostile Marital Interactions, Proinflammatory Cytokine Production, and Wound Healing." Archives of General Psychology, Vol. 62, Dec. 2005.

Approaches to stop worrying:

Psychotherapy

Psychoanalysts try to help people who worry too much by trying to uncover the "root" of their worries. This approach uses psychotherapy to expose key moments that have influenced the development of the patient's personality. The idea is that an understanding of the root cause of their anxiety will make them stop worrying. Unfortunately this approach may produce people who still continue to worry, but are now better informed as to the root causes of their anxiety.

Cognitive Behaviour

This form of therapy sees worry and anxiety as the result of "wrong thinking". The worrier has formed a number of incorrect assumptions about themselves and the world that need to be corrected. Once these corrections have been pointed out the worrier should stop worrying. Although this approach is sometimes successful, there are still a number of people who recognise their wrong thinking but continue to worry anyway.

Thought Stopping

The principle behind thought stopping is simply tell yourself to stop whenever you start to worry. We all know how difficult that is. Telling someone not to think about something immediately makes them think about it. Thought stopping as a technique can often make matters worse. The more you try to stop thinking about something the more you make yourself think about it.

Practical advice to help you stop worrying

Here is a précis of some advice given by Robert L. Leahy, PhD, director of the American Institute for Cognitive Therapy.[18]

> *List your worries* - then analyse them to decide which ones you can influence and which you can't.
>
> *Accept uncertainty* - learn to accept that there are certain situations that are beyond your control.

---

[18] The Worry Cure: Seven Steps to Stop Worry from Stopping You by Robert L. Leahy

Repetition of certain thoughts - can make them lose their power. You may be able to bore yourself into a calmer state of mind.

Learn to confront uncomfortable situations. - If you have a fear of public speaking for example, force yourself to accept a number of public speaking engagements. Forcing yourself to do the things that cause you to worry can stop you from using worry as a coping mechanism. The added bonus is that once you become more proficient as a public speaker the fear of uncertainty will diminish.

Focus on the moment. - Try to take the sense of urgency out of the situation. When we worry we feel a need to resolve the situation immediately to get rid of the worry. Often it is impossible to resolve a worrying situation immediately. When this happens you should try to focus on the here and now, not the resolution of the problem. Take a deep breath read, or listen to music to help stop that feeling of urgency which is only making matters worse.

Remember that things are never as bad as you think they are. - The anticipation of negative events can be worse than your reaction to event when it actually happens. According to Leahy

"Worriers are actually good at handling real problems."

Work with your emotions not against them. - Cry out if you feel you need to, the release can make you feel better.

Talk about your worries. Talking to someone who is sympathetic always helps you feel better about your worries. It is far better to speak to someone that to keep your worries 'bottled up'. Articulating your worries may make you see them in a truer perspective. They may not appear so all consuming once spoken out loud. Speaking to someone, even if they cannot offer any practical advice, provides a form of release. This is where psychotherapy and cognitive behaviour therapy can really help. If you don't want to talk to a therapist talk to a friend.

How to stop yourself from worrying

Given that prevention is better than cure, lets look at some strategies that you can adopt to help prevent yourself from worrying.

Focus on the present. Worriers tend to speculate on possible negative future events. Constantly anticipating the worst possible outcome can provoke a "worry chain" where one worry will spur a "what if," which in turn will spur another worry and another "what if," and so on. Non worriers tend to adopt the attitude that it may never happen, so why worry about it. Staying in the present is fundamental to combating the onset of worry. That's not to say that you shouldn't take sensible precautions to avoid negative outcomes.

Take more chances. Worriers often find it difficult to make decisions. They become indecisive due to the number of potentially negative outcomes they have to take time considering. Taking chances means that you gain more experience of positive outcomes and this enables you to put bad outcomes into a better perspective. Being decisive puts you in control, which stops you feeling like a victim.

Develop a sense of perspective. Try to distance yourself from negative situations so that you can try and see them more objectively. Jason Moser, Ph.D. assistant professor in the Department of Psychology at Michigan State University suggests a simple strategy to help gain perspective. Referring to yourself in the third person when making negative statements can help you to distance yourself. For example instead of saying "I'm going to fail" say "(your name) is going to fail". If you make a number of these third person statements about yourself you will start to see that the worry begins to diminish as these statements do not have the same power those using the term "I".

Become a problem solver not a problem generator. Christine Purdon, a licensed psychologist, professor and executive director of the Centre for Mental Health Research at the University of Waterloo makes the distinction between problem solvers and problem generators. Worriers believe that generating potential problems is a constructive activity. Although identifying potential problems can be helpful on occasions, worriers tend to become stuck in this way of thinking.

Set aside a designated time to worry. This may seem strange. The idea is that you attend to the matter in hand and reserve a time to worry later. The benefit is that you don't have to waste time worrying when you should be concentrating on something else. You have a designated fifteen minute time slot to consider all those negative outcomes. Often the deferment of worries to their time slot will result in the worries disappearing. You have given yourself permission to deal with your worries, while allowing yourself to think about something else at the moment.

Develop the confidence to know that you can handle most situations. One of the problems with worry is that you concentrate on negative outcomes and you also underestimate your ability to deal with them. Worrying undermines your confidence in yourself, it becomes a vicious circle. The more you worry the less confident you feel which makes you worry more. Developing a confident attitude makes you feel more confident, which helps break the cycle.

The SMILE approach to worry and introspection is a long term approach. Repetition of thoughts builds stronger neural connections in your brain. Reducing your worries and negative thoughts reduces the negative neural connections in your brain. Increasing your positive thoughts increases the positive neural connections in your brain. Adopting the SMILE approach is designed to turn a vicious circle into a virtuous circle.

4

LEARNING NEW SKILLS

To be happy you have to learn to like yourself. Learning new skills and setting yourself challenges is an excellent way to boost your self esteem. Moaning and worrying both damage your self esteem. People with high self esteem generally display some of the following:

They like themselves.
They feel valued.
They are able to make decisions and assert themselves.
They believe people like them.
They do not blame themselves for things that are not their fault.
They do not feel guilty for spending time or money on themselves.
They are able to recognise their strengths.

They feel that they deserve to be happy.
They are self confident.

Low self esteem and self doubt, like worrying and moaning rob you of peace of mind. Without a feeling of equanimity it is impossible to be happy. Setting yourself challenges and learning new skills is essential to being happy. Accomplishing new things boosts your self esteem; it makes you more assertive and helps you focus on the positives. The third form of behaviour that the SMILE approach addresses is:

Learn new skills and set yourself challenges.

Why you need to set yourself challenges

There is a paradox associated with setting yourself a challenge. Doing something challenging can be risky, putting yourself at risk is stressful, and stress makes you unhappy. We all tend to avoid unnecessary risks, we seek out the safety associated with avoiding challenging situations. In general people are more fearful than they are courageous. It is only by overcoming challenging situations that we are able to grow, both emotionally and intellectually. For example, you have to risk rejection when you ask someone for a date. You have to volunteer to make a speech to learn to overcome your fear of public speaking. Only by taking risks, can you experience the satisfaction and joy of succeeding in the face of a challenge. The greater the risk, the greater the reward.

The Rewards of Meeting a Challenge.

Eliminates Self Doubt

Success in the face of any challenge begins with the belief that you can succeed. The rigors of the challenge force you to think like a winner. You have to tell yourself that you can do this. The challenge demands that you stay focused and confident, particularly during high-pressure situations so that you can perform at your full potential. The challenge itself forces you to eliminate any feelings of self doubt.

Conquers Your Fears

Challenging situations are inherently fearful and stimulate the stress response. You can learn to overcome your fears by meeting the challenge. Once the challenge has been met, the stress response is replaced by positive feelings of relief and joy. The pleasurable feelings associated with overcoming the stress response can in extreme situations become "addictive", hence the so called 'adrenaline junkie'. In general, overcoming your fears means that when the challenging situation presents itself again you are no longer afraid of it. The challenging situation is no longer challenging and therefore no longer provokes a stress response. For example arachnophobes learn to confront their fear of spiders by confronting spiders in a series of increasingly challenging situations. This is the basis of aversion therapy.

Inspires Courage

Overcoming a challenge, demands courage. When you stand up and volunteer for something that you are fearful of, or nervous about, it takes courage. It is always far easier to keep quiet or make excuses as to why you shouldn't become involved. Reflecting on your courageous behaviour after the event helps boost your self image and your self esteem. The opposite is true when you duck out of the challenge; you feel that you have let yourself down.

Test Your Limits

You never know what you are capable of until you are tested. Even if you fail the test you will learn things about yourself. The true test of character is being able to accept the challenge again even though you have failed in the past. True winners never give up.

Builds Self-Confidence

It is well known that success breeds success. As you overcome more challenges so your confidence and self esteem grow. Your confidence grows as you overcome more and more difficult challenges. You become used to being a winner, and you are able to do things that other people are wary of. You have the self confidence to accept challenges that other people may be afraid to try.

Expands Your Worldview

As a winner, you are not afraid to step out of your comfort zone. Your self confidence and your ever growing number of achievements help change your perspective of what is actually possible. You learn to welcome situations that once provoked fear and self doubt, they have now become opportunities. If you can succeed in one situation that once seemed impossible, why shouldn't you succeed in another?

Teaches You More About Yourself

As well as testing your limits, a challenge teaches you how to behave in certain situations. You learn which methods work best for you, which strategies to adopt to bring about the results you desire. You learn more about yourself, by finding out what works for you and what doesn't. If you don't put yourself in challenging situations you will never have any reason to change the way you act. The same old safe situations will always provoke the same safe behaviour. A challenge demands new ways of behaving. You may find that changing the way you behave, even in safe situations produces better results. If you hadn't accepted the challenge you would never have learned that.

Above all accepting and overcoming a challenge makes you happy. Eliminating self doubt, conquering your fears, acting courageously, becoming self confident are all conducive to making you happy.

Contemporary Philosophers and Happiness

Contemporary philosophers of happiness from Herbert Marcuse to Sonja Lyubomirsky examine the question from a diverse range of perspectives. Starting with the effects of society, through the impact of human needs to how much of our happiness may be genetically determined. Marcuse in "The Affirmative Character of Culture" states that social order is threatened by the tension which develops in society as a result of culture. If this happens, the demand for happiness will cease to be external, and begin to become an object of spiritual contemplation. Marcuse also believes that although society claims to be democratic, it is actually authoritarian. Only certain choices of happiness are available to be purchased, because a few individuals dictate the perceptions of freedom for all. The idea that 'happiness can be bought' is psychologically damaging. actualised, or self fulfilled.

Maslow in his 1943 paper "A Theory of Human Motivation" claimed that there was a hierarchy of needs. Starting at the base, there were physiological needs, then safety, love/belonging, esteem and finally self actualisation. To be truly happy one must reach the top of the pyramid of needs and be self actualised, or self fulfilled.

Happiness and Risk

Accepting a challenge involves risk. Obviously some types of risk are best avoided, for example, reckless behaviour such as drunk driving or excessive gambling. Calculated risks are essential to living a happy and fulfilling life; after all, you take a risk every time you walk out the front door. Risk taking is essential if you are to learn new skills. If you want to be a pilot you will have fly solo one day. In order for something to be risky there has to be an element of danger or a potential loss. The calculation comes when you balance the potential gain against the possible loss. We live in a risk averse society because we all want to be safe. The problem with a risk averse society, is the belief that all risks are necessarily bad. That is not the case; remember some risk is essential for self improvement and happiness.

Learn To Take Positive Risks

Develop Your Risk Tolerance.

A study[19] on self belief and risk taking found that by increasing the level of risk by small amounts you can increase your levels of self belief. As your self belief grows so your tolerance to risk increases. You gradually become more comfortable with higher risk taking behaviour.

Set Your Expectations.

Colin Camerer, a behavioral finance and economics professor at the California Institute of Technology and Elizabeth Phelps, of New York University studied risk and expectations among gamblers. The study published in the "Proceedings of the National Academies of Science" found that those gamblers who were told to pretend that losing was something that happened every day outperformed those that didn't have those expectations. The gamblers who saw losses as something to be expected and acceptable were able to make smarter decisions in high risk situations because they were not so stressed. Ironically, we are usually told that if you want to win think like a winner. It seems that the

---

[19] Krueger, N.F. & Dickson, P. R. (1994). How believing in ourselves influences risk taking: Self-efficacy and opportunity recognition, *Decision Sciences*; *25*, 3, 385-400.

opposite is sometimes true, if you want to stay calm in some high risk situations.

Stay Calm.

Stress is often caused by uncertainty. High risk situations are by their nature full of uncertainty. There are different ways of combating the stress reaction. In some situations telling yourself that the outcome is not important can help you stay calm. In general, self belief and telling yourself that you will succeed helps combat negative thoughts. You will reduce your stress reaction if you manage your self doubts and thereby reduce your feelings of uncertainty.

Become More Risk Aware.

Thinking and learning about risk taking can actually increase your chances of taking positive risks. The more you learn about certain types of risk the more acceptable those risks become. From being totally risk averse in a safety conscious society, you learn that certain types of risk can be a good thing.

It Is All About Balance.

According to Deborah Lupton, professor of Cultural Studies and Cultural Policy at Australia's Charles Strut University, people require both 'routine and risk'. Routine is the opposite of risk, it is familiar and safe. To be happy we all need to find the right balance between the two, which will be different for everyone.

Positive Psychology and Happiness

Positive Psychology[20] is a movement led by psychologist Martin Seligman in the 1990s. Positive Psychology focuses on using scientific understanding and effective intervention in promoting a satisfactory life, rather than focusing on mental illness. Adherents of positive psychology have published many studies on the science of happiness, the two main approaches are:

Neuroscientific – which looks at happiness from a physiological perspective, studying brain chemistry for example, using techniques such as brain imaging to try and understand what makes us happy or depressed.

Evolutionary – which attempts to understand the evolutionary advantages of positive and negative states of mind. How does being happy or depressed improve our ability to survive and reproduce?

---

[20] https://en.wikipedia.org/wiki/Positive_psychology

*Martin Seligman in his book "Flourish"[21] outlines five elements he considers necessary for well-being, using the mnemonic P.E.R.M.A: **P**ositive emotion, **E**ngagement, **R**elationships, **M**eaning, and **A**chievement. Another concept central to Positive Psychology is Flow introduced by Mihály Csíkszentmihályi. Flow, sometimes referred to as being "in the zone", is a mental state where one is fully immersed in a particular activity. Flow, sometimes referred to as being "in the zone", is a mental state where one is fully immersed in a particular activity. Flow describes a state where one is totally focused, energised and fully involved in the task in hand.*

Sonja Lyubomirsky in "The How of Happiness" asserts that happiness is 50 percent genetically determined and 10 percent the result of circumstances, the remaining 40 percent is under our own control.

21

https://books.google.co.uk/books?id=mQ4_UwcCojUC&redir_esc=y

To try to sum up the philosophy of happiness; it began with equating the idea of happiness with leading a good life. In the middle ages, happiness meant observing religious practice. Early modern philosophers examined the subjective nature of happiness looking for principles or laws of happiness based on cultural or biological factors. More recently the focus has been on trying to gain a scientific understanding of happiness.

Risk And The Brain

Specific areas of your brain are associated with risky behaviour. Studies with rats at Stanford University found activity in this area of the brain determined whether animals decided to engage in a risky activity or not. According to Karl Deisseroth, Professor of Bioengineering and Psychiatry at Stanford University, "Humans and rats have similar brain structures." Deisseroth stated "We found that a drug known to increase risk preference in people had the same effect on the rats. So every indication is that these findings are relevant to humans."

Research[22] on risky behaviour in rats focused on the reward system. A deep brain structure known as the ventral tegmental is linked to another structure in the forebrain called the nucleus accumbens. Neurons in this link secrete dopamine which attaches itself to receptors in the nucleus accumbens. Previous research, including human brain-imaging by co author of the study Professor Brian Knutson had shown increased activity in the nucleus accumbens when people were considering taking risks. The study focused on activity in nerve cells during the decision making process. Rats were taught to press a lever to deliver a reward of sugary

[22] Nucleus accumbens D2R cells signal prior outcomes and control risky decision-making
KA Zalocusky, C Ramakrishnan, TN Lerner... - Nature, 2016

water. The rats were then given a choice, one lever delivered a consistent reward, the other lever generally delivered a smaller dose of sugary water, but occasionally delivered a very large dose. They found that for about one second after the trial had begun, but before any levers were pressed that there was significant activity in the nucleus accumbens of risk averse rats but not risk seeking rats. Researchers found that by stimulating activity in the nucleus accumbens of risk seeking rats, it would make them risk averse. They could reverse the rats behaviour by delivering a drug known to promote more risky behaviour in humans to the risk averse rats to make them behave in a more risky fashion. Deisseroth concluded "It looks as though we have found a brain signal that, in most individuals, corresponds to a memory of a failed risky choice,"

Setting Goals To Make You Happy

The very act of goal setting can make you happy. Goal setting makes you think of positive outcomes that you want to achieve, which releases dopamine into your brain which makes you happy. Goal setting makes you happy because goals focus your attention on things that interest you or bring you pleasure. Goals can provide a sense of meaning and purpose to your life. Accomplishing your goals provides you with a sense of achievement, building your self confidence and self esteem. Goals provide you with an investment in your own your future.

Goal Setting Theory

A study[23] in 2007 suggested that there were two types of goal one of which is associated with happiness and the other which may be detrimental to making you happy. Zero sum goals are self centred goals based on your own desires. Non zero sum goals include the welfare of other people as well as yourself. The study found that the zero sum goals tended to be detrimental in promoting individual happiness, in the form of life satisfaction. The fact that theses goals tended to focus on material gains was cited as the main cause. The researchers in the 2007 study do not claim that you shouldn't focus on trying to achieve your personal goals but that you should try to include the welfare of other people in your goals.

---

[23] Headey, B. (2007 July 3). Life goals matter to happiness: A revision of set-point theory. *Springer Science and Business Media.* http://link.springer.com/article/10.1007%2Fs11205-007-9138-y#/page-1Mehta, M. (2013 January 3). Why our brains like short-term goals. *Entrepreneur.* http://www.entrepreneur.com/article/225356

Research by Ken Sheldon[24] on intrinsic and extrinsic goals found similar results, where the intrinsic goals were said to lead to long term happiness. Extrinsic goals were focused on financial success, attractiveness/image, popularity and conformity. Intrinsic goals were based on self acceptance, community feeling affiliation and physical fitness.

One of the paradoxes of happiness is the belief that trying too hard to make yourself happy can lead to unhappiness. Unrealistic expectations of how happy you can be, and vague notions of how to achieve it, may be the cause of this belief. Jennifer Aaker in a study[25] seeking to identify the results of abstract versus concrete goal setting on happiness stated

"Although the desire for personal happiness may be clear, the path to achieving it is indefinite...

...One reason for this hazy route to happiness is that although people often think they know what leads

---

[24] Sheldon, K., Gunz, A., Nichols, C., & Ferguson, Y. (2010). Extrinsic value orientation and affective forecasting: Overestimating the rewards, underestimating the costs. http://sdtheory.s3.amazonaws.com/SDT/documents/2010_Shel donGunzNicholsFerguson_JOP.pdf

[25]

http://www.sciencedirect.com/science/article/pii/S0022103114 000444 to happiness, their predictions about what will make them happy are often inaccurate."

The study conducted six experiments to measure individual's expectations of happiness while carrying out a number of concrete and more abstract tasks. One experiment consisted of two groups; one group had the task of making someone happy and the other of simply making someone smile. To complete the tasks both groups tried a number of different strategies, including giving a gift, telling a joke showing a funny video and giving someone food. They found that those with the concrete task, of making someone smile made themselves happier than those with the more abstract task of trying to make someone happy. Although both tasks were clearly related the concrete task was easier to achieve. Participants in the experiments had predicted no difference in the effects on personal happiness of both tasks. When the participants considered both tasks simultaneously they predicted that the abstract task would lead to greater happiness than the concrete task.

What makes a good goal?

Ideally you should seek to have a mixture of long term, short term and possibly day to day goals. It is often a good idea to break down your long term goals into a number of short term goals to make them achievable and manageable. You will boost your own happiness if your goals are supported by other people in your life. Try to make your short term goals consistent with your long term goals, even when they are not a part of the long term goal. Your goals not only determine your actions, they also affect the amount of effort you put into achieving them and how persistent you are in try to achieve them.

S.M.A.R.T goals

The mnemonic acronym, S.M.A.R.T generally associated with goal setting was first used by George T. Doran in the November 1981 issue of "Management Review". An objective or goal should be:

Specific – target a specific area for improvement.

Measurable – quantify or at least suggest an I ndicator of progress.

Assignable – specify who will do it.

Realistic – state what results can realistically be achieved, given available resources.

Time-related – specify when the result(s) can be achieved.

Other variations include Strategic, Motivating, Achievable, Agreed, Action-oriented, Ambitious, Aligned with other goals, Relevant, Realistic, Resourced, Reasonable, Results-based, Time-bound, Trackable, Time-based, Time limited, Time/cost limited, Timely, Time-sensitive and Timeframe.

Goal Setting and Optimism

It is important to be positive when setting goals. A goal should enable you to achieve a positive outcome rather than avoid a negative one. An optimistic approach to life in general has been shown[26] to promote a sense of well being. Optimism helps you to be more proactive when setbacks occur. Optimists tend to look for solutions rather than ignore problems when they arise. Although optimism is important you should remember not to be overly optimistic. It is important to set realistic goals that will stretch you but which you can achieve. Unrealistically high expectations will only lead to failure and a sense of disappointment.

---

[26]] Carver, C.S., Scheier, M.F., Miller, C.J., & Fulford, D. (2009). Optimism. In S.J.Lopez & C.R. Snyder (Eds.) Oxford Handbook of Positive Psychology. NY: Oxford University Press.

Practical Advice on Goal Setting

1. Decide what you want to achieve. Start with something that is stretching but achievable; goals that stretch you can be motivating, as long they are not too easy or too difficult.
2. Apply the SMART definition to your goal.
3. Write down your goal. This is important; you are more likely to achieve your goal if you write it down. Writing it down makes it concrete and not just an abstract idea in your head. Writing it down will help you to be more persistent in the face of future setbacks.
4. Tell someone what your goal is. Telling someone what your goal is has the same effect as writing it down, with the added benefit someone else will now know if fail or decide to give up. The thought of being regarded as a failure will give you a greater incentive top succeed. .
5. Break your goal down if you can. If you have set yourself a big goal, it is obviously essential to break it down into achievable stages, each a goal in itself. Sometimes you can break your short term goals down, into smaller steps which will help you to achieve your desired end. Achieving lots of smaller goals keeps you on track to achieve your

major goal always look to see i9f you can break any goal down into easier stages.

6. Decide your first step. There is no point in setting a goal if you don't decide to carry it out. Don't fool yourself that you have done all the work in deciding to do something; you actually have to start doing it.

7. Be persistent. I'm sure that you will have heard of the famous Thomas Eddison quote "Genius is one percent inspiration, ninety-nine percent perspiration." Achieving your goals is all about being persistent. When you have those moments of self doubt you will be pleased that you wrote down your objective and told someone about it. Succeeding in the face of setbacks, problems and frustrations is all part of the process and a necessary part which makes the end achievement all the more satisfying.

8. Celebrate your success. Take the time to enjoy your success, you will have earned it. Thank all those people that helped and supported you. Consider all those things that you enjoyed and learned during the process. Think about the things that you will be able to do better next time, then decide what you want to achieve next.

The first two rules associated with the SMILE approach seek to reduce negative behaviour. Eliminating negative behaviour, results in positive behaviour, which in turn results in positive thoughts and attitudes, which become habitual through repetition. The third rule seeks to promote positive behaviour in its own right. Learning new skills and overcoming challenges are both enjoyable experiences. Enjoyable experiences stimulate the release of neurotransmitters such as dopamine and endorphins into your body. Put simply dopamine tends to be involved in reinforcing behaviour and endorphins are considered to be your body's natural "feel good chemicals". Neurotransmitters aid the transmission of electrical impulses in your brain. The repetition of certain thoughts and behaviours strengthens the associated connections in your brain making certain behaviours more habitual. Making happiness a habit, is of course central to the SMILE approach.

JEREMY KITT

5

EMPATHY

The final behaviour to be addressed by the SMILE approach is empathy. Empathy is the ability to understand and share the feelings and emotions of other people. Empathy is different from sympathy which means feeling sorry for someone. Empathy is a subjective experience; it is looking at the world from another person's point of view. How does feeling empathy for someone make you feel happy? Well the answer is that by looking at the world from another person's perspective you start to look for the good in people and not just those things which annoy you. This brings us to my rule associated with empathy.

Try to look for the good in people, (particularly those who annoy you.)

The strange thing about trying to find the good in people is that by doing so, you actually start to like those people more. You are always more forgiving of people you like.

The opposite is true of people you dislike; every slightly irritating action or comment they make reinforces your dislike of them. Try it yourself...Pick someone who slightly irritates you and try to cast everything they say or do in the best possible light. Very quickly you will find that they don't appear to be quite so annoying.

One of the main causes of unhappiness is the way other people treat you. We are all affected by the comments and actions of other people, both positively and negatively. If you can do something to reduce the negative effect that these have on you then in principle you should feel happier. One of the main objections to this process is that it is too difficult to do. It may be difficult to do, just as it can be difficult to stop moaning or stop worrying, but it is worth trying. Remember you are doing this for your own happiness. If you make the annoying person happy and as a result they are more pleasant towards you, then their happiness is an added bonus.

Just because you are looking for the good in someone doesn't mean you have to agree with them or capitulate to their point of view. You are trying to be more understanding and more compassionate towards them without being condescending. You can empathise with someone without agreeing with them. One thing you should avoid is to voice your 'insights' or understanding of the causes of their irritating ways to the person in question. Use your insights into their behaviour as a mental crutch to remind you to be pleasant whenever they irritate you.

People generally respond positively if you go out of your way to be pleasant to them. They may be suspicious at first, depending on how you have treated each other in the past. You may object that you are not very good at understanding other people. Any insights that you may think you have about their behaviour and attitudes may be wrong. That doesn't matter. In fact your insights about their behaviour may be wrong, particularly if you do not know anything about their past life. It doesn't matter if your 'insights' are wrong, you are not trying to offer them therapy, the insights are for your own use not theirs. Remember you are not trying to judge people; you are just trying to understand them better so that you will not find them so annoying.

Another objection to this approach is that it is all a bit 'Pollyanna-ish'. Pollyanna is a somewhat annoying fictional character who insists in seeing the best in everyone. Pollyanna is overly cheerful about everything and is nearly always blinkered regarding other people's malicious intentions. Obviously people sometimes act out of malice, greed, jealousy, ambition, ignorance, incompetence, etc. Trying to see the good in people doesn't mean that you should ignore the fact that some people are liars, cheats and troublemakers. This isn't a perfect world and trying to see the good in others is not always possible.

Trying to see the best in people creates a virtuous circle; looking for the best in others, brings out the best in them. It is a self fulfilling prophecy. The opposite is also true. Looking for the worst in others and judging them brings out the worst in them, creating a vicious circle. Your negative expectations are confirmed by behaviour which you are looking at from a judgemental, negative perspective. Looking for the good in others is not always about seeing the world through rose tinted glasses.

Does Everyone Want to be Happy?

We take it as read that everyone wants to be happy. Happiness is the highest goal in the West. All other objectives such as the pursuit of wealth, fame, personal enlightenment or public approbation are all subservient to the ultimate goal - to be happy. In fact studies[27] indicate that positive events such as winning the vast sums of money and negative events such as becoming disabled in an accident do not significantly affect an individual's long-term levels of happiness. On the other hand, failure to achieve happiness is often perceived as a major failure in life. It appears that other cultures may not share our obsession with happiness.

---

[27] studies of lottery winners and other individuals at the top of their game

Sometimes looking for the good in others can be just a matter of taking off those "cynical glasses". Everyone has some positive character traits.

Cultural Differences in Approaches to Happiness

In a study[28] of the cultural differences between American and Taiwanese students in their approach to happiness, happiness was defined as experiencing pleasure, positive emotion, or success. Students were asked for their opinions on the nature of happiness. The American students considered happiness to be the highest value and supreme goal in their lives. Taiwanese participants made no such statements.

---

[28] http://link.springer.com/article/10.1007/s10902-004-8789-5

A number of studies[29][30][31] have concluded that happiness is less valued in Eastern cultures than Western ones. The reason may be the different value placed on emotions by both societies. One example of how this difference manifests itself is in the public display of emotions. There are a number of social situations in which East Asians may be more inclined than Westerners to feel it inappropriate to express happiness.[32]

---

[29] https://www.ncbi.nlm.nih.gov/pubmed/11708563

[30]
http://www2.psych.ubc.ca/~heine/docs/2001compenhance.pdf

[31]http://www.gruberpeplab.com/teaching/psych131_fall2013/documents/4.1_Kitayama2006_CulturalAffordances.pdf

[32]
http://www.danweijers.com/pdf/Aversion%20to%20happiness%20across%20cultures-A%20review%20of%20where%20and%20why%20people%20are%20averse%20to%20happiness.pdf

Positive Character Traits To Look For

Positive Intentions.

Trying to understand the reason people are behaving in a particular way rather than the effects of that behaviour on you. For example, you share a piece of sensitive information with someone who quickly changes the subject. Their behaviour may seem insensitive to you at first until you realise that they are just uncomfortable with the news. An argumentative teenager may be looking for attention because they have low self esteem.

Hidden Abilities.

We are often quick to judge others. It is as if by making others look bad, we will look good in comparison. This is rarely the case. The problem with judging others is that we put a convenient label on them. X is a real bore, or Y is a fusspot. These labels stop us from uncovering other peoples' talents and abilities. Labels narrowly define them in a negative way. Once you stop using these labels and start trying to understand other people, then their hidden talents start to reveal themselves. People may relax more if they feel that they are no longer pigeonholed. Once people relax, it becomes easier for them to display any hidden abilities.

Positive Character Traits.

As with hidden abilities, so you should learn to look for positive character traits. Look for virtues in those around you rather than faults. The more open and positive we are to other people so the easier it is to identify virtues such as determination, generosity, kindness, patience, tenacity, honesty, fairness, compassion etc.

Arguments Against Being Happy?

Joshanloo and Weijers of Victoria University of Wellington in their paper "Aversion to happiness across cultures"[33] outline four arguments against trying to be happy:

Being happy makes it more likely that bad things will happen to you

Some people believe that bad things such as unhappiness, suffering, and death tend to happen more to happy people. It is better to be neither happy nor sad, but to be neutral to avoid the unhappiness that is thought to occur as a result of being too happy. Taoists for example believe in balance and that things tend to revert to their opposite, therefore happiness can provoke unhappiness and vice versa. A study[34] found that when Americans and Chinese were shown graphs depicting various trends over the course of a life, the Chinese tended to pick the graphs that showed the

---

[33]

http://www.danweijers.com/pdf/Aversion%20to%20happiness%20across%20cultures-A%20review%20of%20where%20and%20why%20people%20are%20averse%20to%20happiness.pdf

[34] http://pss.sagepub.com/content/12/6/450.short

trend for happiness reverting or oscillating. .There is a Christian belief that happiness in the form of worldly pleasures can lead one away from God. Medieval Christians believed that an excess of worldly happiness could lead to eternal damnation. Western expressions such as "after happiness, there comes a fall" and "what goes up must come down" express a similar belief.

Being happy makes you a worse person

This is the belief that being happy makes you morally bad. Muslims tend to be critical of people who are too happy. The Quran states "avoid much laughter, for much laughter deadens the heart" (Quran, 5:87). The Shiites believe that happiness is associated with shallowness, foolishness, and vulgarity. Happiness is a distraction from God. In the West there is a belief that happy people are superficial and can't be taken seriously. Happy people are seen as shallow and can't be serious intellectuals. There is a view that oppressed minorities avoid happiness, as it can make them weak, or less motivated to fight oppression. There is also a cultural myth that unhappy people are more creative than happy people, to produce great art you must suffer.

Expressing happiness is bad for you and others

This is the view that talking about being happy, smiling or laughing too much, or indeed any overt expression is bad not only for the person expressing the happiness but for others around them as well. In some Eastern cultures overt displays of happiness or success may generate feelings of envy in others which could lead to feelings of guilt and disharmony. In Russia expressions of happiness or success were often seen as a cause of envy, suspicion and resentment in others[35]. There is a belief in Russia that

---

[35] Lyubomirsky (2000).In the pursuit of happiness: Comparing the U.S. and Russia. Paper presented at the Annual Meeting of the Society of Experimental Social Psychology, Atlanta, Georgia.(Sumposium titled "Happiness, Hope, Optimism and Maturity: Social Psychological Approaches to Human Strengths.")

anyone who is happy or successful may have used immoral means to achieve them. In the West demonstrations of extreme happiness or success are generally believed to be a bad thing in case they provoke feelings of envy in others.

Pursuing happiness is bad for you and others

In many cultures there are warnings about pursuing certain types of pleasure, because they are deemed to be bad for both the pursuer and those around them. Many believe that the pursuit of pleasure in itself is a bad thing and can lead to cruelty, violence pride and greed. The pursuit of pleasure can also lead to neglect of ones duties. It has been argued that the active pursuit of happiness requires a great deal of effort, which impedes the carefree attitude necessary to appreciate happiness. This has been called the Paradox of Happiness; the active pursuit of happiness is more likely to lead to unhappiness.

Bringing Out The Best In Others

Give others the benefit of the doubt. Try to believe in other people, particularly when they fail, or suffer from self doubt.

Develop an open mind. We are all different and learning to embrace those differences helps create a happy productive environment. We tend to like people that we consider to be similar to ourselves. This creates a problem, namely that restricting the people you like to a certain type, means that you miss out on opportunities to get to know a whole range of interesting people. Let me give you an example. During WW2 the British broke the German enigma codes which shortened the war by years. The Nazis could never have done this because the people who actually broke those codes were the very people that they condemned as socially unacceptable misfits. Don't let your biases and prejudices get in the way.

Be persistent. It may not be easy to look for the positive in others. You may find it easier not to bother or to always see the negative. It takes effort and persistence to find the best in other people.

How To Be The Sort Of Person That Other People Will Like

The other side of the coin to trying to find the best in other people is trying to find the best in yourself. There are a lot of self help books which to try to help you become more popular, which all began with Dale Carnegie's "How to Win Friends and Influence People" published in 1936. Here are a few suggestions of things that you can do to become the sort of person that other people will like:

Get to know yourself. Be positive and list your best personal qualities. You can also list your failings and weaknesses as areas to work on. This is where introspection may be able to help. Decide on the type of person that you would like to be, and start trying to be that type of person. For example, you may see yourself as a leader, or someone who has creative ideas or someone who is steadfast and reliable, someone that people can depend on in a crisis.

Try not to seek out other peoples' approval. If you try to change yourself just to be popular, you are likely to fail. Other people will quickly see through that ploy. You run the risk of catering to other people's expectations of how you should behave instead of being true to yourself. You should still try to set a good example in the way that you behave, but do it for the right reasons.

Be true to yourself. That means not pretending to be someone that you are not. Try to live your life according to your values and back up your words with your actions. Other people will trust you if you are sincere in the things you say and do. Just as you shouldn't try to court popularity, so you should try not to judge other people's behaviour.

Develop your own self esteem. If you want other people to like you, you have to learn to like yourself. If you have taken the time to get to know yourself, and are behaving in a way that is consistent with your values, that will help build your self esteem. If you are suffering from low self esteem try to do things that make you feel better about yourself. Try to create a virtuous circle whereby doing things that you are good at, reinforces positive feelings about yourself, which makes you want to do more things you are good at. Talk about yourself in a positive way and reward yourself when you succeed.

Be positive. Just as with moaning and worrying, it can be easy to slip into a negative way of thinking. Guard against being too negative. It is easy to pretend you are just being wise and that your cynicism is your ability to see what is really happening. The problem is that it can be habit forming so remember to take off those "cynical glasses".

Develop your communication skills. Try to be a good listener. People like it when you pay attention to them. In a lot of conversations there tends to be an unwritten agreement, I'll put up with what you have to say if you listen to me. It's a kind of quid pro quo whereby instead of listening to the other person you are looking for cues in what they say so that you can speak. Try really listening to what they are saying and encourage them by asking relevant questions. When you speak, do so with confidence and conviction. If you have worked on being positive and developing your self esteem then this will help. Try to be relaxed when you speak, to put other people at ease. If you are true to yourself and are not openly seeking the approval of others then people will be more likely to trust what you have to say.

Empathising and looking for the good in other people is the final rule associated with the SMILE approach to happiness. Each of the four rules will work to promote your happiness in its own right, but collectively they help reinforce each other to strengthen the results. You may be asking yourself why there are only four rules; surely there are other positive behaviours that you could adopt to help promote your own happiness. Let me answer that question by saying that the number of behaviours and associated rules has been deliberately kept as low as possible to make them easier to follow and to remember. Each of the four rules is broad enough to encompass any number of different situations, but focused enough to enable you to use it as a practical guide in any particular situation.

There are no doubt, many other behaviours that you could and should adopt to promote your happiness. The central aim of the SMILE approach is to make your happiness become habitual, that is only achieved through repetition. If you adopt too many new behaviours, not only does the process become unwieldy, but you may end up diluting the habit forming attitudes and behaviours. In any process of change it is best to focus on a few changes to begin with. Changing everything at once often ends in failure.

In the next chapter I will discuss how to implement the SMILE approach to change your behaviour.

JEREMY KITT

.

6

INDIVIDUAL HAPPINESS

You have now been introduced to the four rules associated with the SMILE approach to promoting individual happiness. Let's take a minute for a brief recap before we explore how you can use SMILE to change your behaviour and some of the benefits of doing so.

Each of the four rules outlined in the SMILE method are designed to promote individual happiness:

> 1. *'Stop Moaning'* and you will begin to foster a more positive attitude to life.

> 2. *'Don't worry about things that you can't do anything about, if you can do something, then do it.'* If you cannot do anything to improve your situation, try to manage your level of worry. Articulating your worries to

someone else, even if they can't offer any solutions can help vent your frustrations and fears. Try not to keep your worries to yourself; it is too easy to magnify them. Try to control your worries, don't let them control you.

3. *'Learn new skills and set yourself challenges'* to develop your self-confidence and boost your self esteem.

4. *'Try to look for the good in people,' (particularly those who annoy you.)* At first sight this rule may look as if it were designed to promote happiness in other people. Its primary aim is to make you feel happier. If you are well disposed towards someone who usually irritates or annoys you, the chances are they will be pleasant in return. At first this may seem like an act, but if you persevere you may find that you genuinely come to like that other person.

All four rules in the SMILE method are simple to understand but can be very difficult to follow. To be happy takes work. You need to adjust your behaviour and your attitudes. Each of the rules will promote your happiness if taken in isolation, but obviously work better when you use them all together. One rule can help reinforce another; boosting your self confidence and self esteem will make it easier to look for the good in others, for example. Managing your worries will make it easier to stop moaning.

If you fail, learn by your failures and try to do better next time. Set yourself challenges, for example you might decide to try to win over, someone you know dislikes you. Don't expect to be able to change immediately, it will take time. Gradually as you adopt the new behaviours and positive attitude so your whole personality will change. You will become happier and more satisfied with your life.

Changing Your Behaviour

People generally don't like change. Newton's, first law of motion states: "A body at rest tends to remain at rest. A body in motion tends to stay in motion. Bodies will continue in their current state, whether at rest or in motion, unless acted on by a greater outside force." Sport psychologist, Dr Jim Taylor, Adjunct Professor at the University of San

Francisco proposed[36] his own law of human inertia: "The tendency of people, having once established a life trajectory, to continue on that course unless acted on by a greater force." According to Taylor we are resistant to change because of behaviour we learned at an earlier age, which we continue to manifest even though that behaviour may not be in our best interest. Examples of such behaviour may be resentment of authority, making it hard to socialise, low self esteem making it hard to assert yourself. Change is difficult, particularly self change, to be successful you need to be persistent.

How To Make Changes In Your Life:

Simplify the process. Break down the changes into the smallest elements possible. You are more likely to be successful taking lots of small steps than one or two gigantic leaps. You could try setting yourself small achievable targets to begin with, such as having a conversation with someone who you know dislikes you as the first step in trying to that person like you.

Do not fear the unknown. It is easier to stick to tried and tested behaviour than try something

---

[36] http://www.huffingtonpost.com/dr-jim-taylor/asteroids-law-human-inertia_b_1116917.html

new. To overcome this reluctance it is necessary to examine the consequences of change, prepare yourself and set yourself realistic goals. Think about how you have reacted to new situations in the past and try to plan for better outcomes in the future.

Make positive changes. Learn to enjoy the act of change, admire the outcome and reward yourself. Give yourself a small reward for each step you achieve.

Prepare for problems. Learn from your setbacks.

Take it slowly. Taking changes at a slower pace will allow you to better acclimatise yourself to the changes. Allow your changes to become automatic behaviours. Remember SMILE is an ongoing process; it is all about the repetition of positive attitudes and behaviour.

Take control. Controlling the process of change, means monitoring your behaviour. You can use introspection to monitor your feelings and attitudes during the process. Ask for feedback from friends; how did they react when you said or did something new? Analysing your new behaviour will help you to understand the types of behaviour that will bring about positive outcomes for you.

Plan your changes. To be successful try to structure your changes. It makes them easier to predict and monitor. Spontaneity may be a good thing on some occasions, but it increases your chances of failing when trying to make lasting change. Structure allows you to identify what works for you, and repeat it in different circumstances.

Practice. Practise new approaches so you can prepare for possible outcomes. Think through your strategies and try them out in different situations. Ensure that your new behaviour becomes permanent by repeating it over and over again.

The Benefits of Happiness

There are obvious benefits associated with being happy, such as feelings of well being and contentment, increased self confidence and self esteem. The causal relationship between happiness and potential benefits is unclear. For example, it is unclear whether giving makes you happy, which it generally does, or whether happy people give more, which they generally do. The answer is that it is probably a combination of both.

Here are some of the other benefits associated with being happy:

Happy People Are More Successful.

A report[37] by psychologists Sonja Lyubomirsky, Laura King, and Ed Diener, asked the question "Does Happiness lead to success?" The report encompassed numerous studies using three types of evidence; cross-sectional, longitudinal and experimental. They concluded that happy individuals are successful across multiple life domains, including marriage, friendship, income, work performance, and health. Happiness leads to success.

Happy People Have More Friends.

A study[38] of 222 undergraduates found that very happy people were highly social, and had stronger romantic and other social relationships than less happy groups. When using the Minnesota

---

[37] http://sonjalyubomirsky.com/wp-content/themes/sonjalyubomirsky/papers/LKDinpress.pdf

[38] http://pss.sagepub.com/content/13/1/81.abstract

Multiphasic Personality Inventory[39], a widely used psychometric test used to assess personality and psychopathology, they also found that happy people were more extroverted, more agreeable, and less neurotic.

Happiness and Altruism

Numerous studies[40] have found a link between happiness and altruism. Happy people tend to give more to charity, are more willing to help others and volunteer more, than unhappy people.

Happiness and Creativity

A study[41] in 2006 found that being in a positive frame of mind can make you more creative. Dr. Adam Anderson, author of the study stated; "having a positive mood affects your attention…. it can broaden your visual field, literally".

39

https://en.wikipedia.org/wiki/Minnesota_Multiphasic_Personality_Inventory

40

http://link.springer.com/article/10.1207/s15327558ijbm1202_4

[41] http://www.pnas.org/content/104/1/383.full

Anderson asked volunteers to solve two types of problem, a creative problem which required word associations and a visual problem that required ignoring distracting information. Volunteers listened to either happy or sad music, and were asked to think about happy or sad things. They found that volunteers performed well on creative problem-solving tasks when in a happy frame of mind.

"People who are in a very good mood may just notice a lot, they are attentive to their environment, so they may be more attentive to the distracters as well," said Dr. Dan McAdams, professor of psychology at Northwestern University in Chicago. Dr. Robert Maurer, a staff psychologist at Santa Monica-UCLA Medical Center has pointed out that the amygdala could have a big effect on creativity. The part of the brain called the amygdala is associated with the fear response, which can affect that part of the brain which is associated with creativity. As Dr Maurer puts it "When you are happy, the amygdala is quiet so that you can be more creative".

Although a positive mood may be beneficial in solving creative problems, Anderson's study also found that it was detrimental when trying to solve distracting problems. In the study happy volunteers performed poorly on the visual problems, which were distracting. Anderson concluded that being happy was distracting in itself, which made it doubly difficult to perform well on a distracting task. Negative moods may be better when trying to solve a problem requiring focus. According to Anderson "a negative mood results in tunnel vision, making you focus on just the things you are anxious about... everything else falls out of this focus and doesn't matter."

Happy People Have More Meaningful Conversations

In a 2010 study[42], Matthias Mehl, a psychologist at the University of Arizona, found that happy people spent more time having deep conversations than engaging in small talk. 79 students (32 men and 47 women) volunteered to wear an electronically activated recorder with a microphone on their lapel that recorded 30-second snippets of conversation every 12.5 minutes for four days. The recordings

---

[42]

http://www.psychologicalscience.org/media/releases/2010/mehl.cfm

were then classified as small talk or substantive talk. Small talk included talk about the weather or having watched a TV show, while substantive talk included talk about current affairs, philosophy, the difference between Baptists and Catholics or the role of education. Some conversations were practical and didn't fit either category.

Over all, about a third of all conversation was ranked as substantive, and about a fifth consisted of small talk. Mehl asked the students to report on their own levels of satisfaction with life, as well as using other measures of happiness, including reports of others who knew them. Mehl found that the happiest person in the group had twice as many substantive conversations, and only one-third of the amount of small talk as the unhappiest. According to Mehl the happiest person spent 45.9 % of the each day's conversations in substantive conversation compared to the unhappiest person who spent 21.8 % of the each day's conversations in substantive conversation.

Happiness and Life Expectancy

A report[43] published in the "Proceedings of the National Academy of Sciences" in the UK claimed that older people who said they were happy were less likely to die over a five-year period. Respondents aged between 52 and 79 were divided into three groups, depending on how happy they claimed to be. Five years later when they examined the mortality rates of the three groups they found only 4% of the happiest group had died, compared to 5% in the middle group and 7% in the unhappy group. When other factors were accounted for such as age, depression, chronic diseases, health behaviours (such as exercise and alcohol consumption), and socio-economic factors, they concluded that the happiest people had a 35% lower risk of dying during the study than those who said they were less happy.

A major new study[44] found no evidence of any relationship between happiness and life expectancy.

43

http://www.sciencedirect.com/science/article/pii/S0140673613614890

[44] http://www.thelancet.com/journals/lancet/article/PIIS0140-6736(15)01087-9/abstract

The study, conducted by Oxford University researchers over ten years, focused on nearly one million women in the UK around the age of 60. They found that although poor health made people unhappy, and that poor health affected life expectancy, there was no evidence that unhappiness in itself made people's lives shorter. Respondents were asked to rate their own health, happiness, stress, feelings of control and whether they felt relaxed. Five out of six said they were generally happy, 44% said they were usually happy and 39% said they were happy most of the time. 17% said that they were unhappy. The questionnaire was repeated with a random sample one year later with similar results. During the ten years of the study over 31,000 respondents died. However the death rates among those who claimed to be unhappy were no higher than those who said they were unhappy.

Happiness and Heart Disease

A study[45] by Laura Kubzansky, HSPH associate professor of society, human development, and health at Harvard published in 2007 found that a

---

[45] https://www.ncbi.nlm.nih.gov/pubmed/17199060

positive attitude appeared to reduce the risk of coronary heart disease.

Kubzansky studied the lives of over 6,000 men and women aged 25 to 74 for 20 years. She found that certain personal attributes help some people reduce the number of diseases such as heart attacks, strokes, diabetes, and depression. The attributes in question are:

> Emotional vitality - sense of enthusiasm, hopefulness and engagement.

> Optimism – having a positive outlook.

> Being good at "self-regulation" - the ability to recover from stressful challenges and knowing that things will get better and the adoption of a healthy lifestyle.

Steptoe and Wardle of University College London in their 2005 study[46] found a relationship between happiness and lower heart rate and blood pressure. Respondents were asked to rate their happiness over 30 times in one day and then repeat the exercise three years later. They found that those who claimed to be happiest on the first

---

[46] https://www.ncbi.nlm.nih.gov/pubmed/16213629

questionnaire had a lower heart rate on the follow-up three years later (about six beats per minute slower). The happiest participants during the second questionnaire also had lower blood pressure.

Happiness can also affect something called heart rate variability, that is the time between heart beats. Reduced heart rate variability is associated with a number of conditions, including heart failure and diabetic neuropathy. A 2008 study[47] asked 76 patients suspected to be suffering coronary artery disease to rate their happiness on a particular day. The respondent's hearts were then tested on the same day. Those who claimed to be happiest were found to have better heart rate variability.

---

[47] https://www.ncbi.nlm.nih.gov/pubmed/18941130

Is Happiness a Right?

According to Joshanloo and Weijers of Victoria University the very idea of happiness is quite a modern concept. In 1794 the French revolutionary Saint-Just stated "Happiness is a new idea in Europe." The concept of happiness was one of the new ideas that helped spawn both the French Revolution and the creation of the United States of America. The Declaration of Independence states:

"We hold these truths to be self-evident, that all men are created equal, that they are endowed by their creator with certain inalienable Rights, that among these are Life, Liberty and the pursuit of Happiness."

Thomas Jefferson, Declaration of Independence

According to the Declaration of Independence all men and presumably women have the right to pursue happiness. . You won't be surprised to learn that the defence, "that I only committed this crime in the pursuit of happiness" has no binding effect in the courts in the USA or elsewhere. The Declaration of Independence is of course concerned with international law and not domestic law . The *document outlines the relationships between States and in particular the British Crown and the newly formed United States. The right to the "pursuit of happiness" is listed among a number of grievances against King George, in an attempt to get other countries to recognise the legitimacy of the Unites States.*

Happiness and Your Immune System

A study[48] in 2003 of 350 adults who were exposed to the common cold found that subjects who expressed the most positive emotions were less likely to develop a cold. Subjects were questioned on six separate occasions over a two week period. They were asked how much they had experienced nine positive emotions on each occasion. The emotions included such things as how energetic they felt, how pleased, how calm they felt.

After a period of five days in quarantine, they found that the subjects who expressed the most positive emotions were less likely to develop a cold. A follow up study[49] in 2006 by some of the same researchers looked at the relationship between happiness and sickness. 81 subjects were given the hepatitis B vaccine. The vaccine was administered in two doses, after the first dose the subjects were asked to rate themselves on the same nine positive emotions as the earlier study. Subjects who rated their positive emotions higher were found to have nearly twice as many antibodies in response to the vaccine than

---

[48] https://www.ncbi.nlm.nih.gov/pubmed/12883117

[49]

http://www.sciencedirect.com/science/article/pii/S0889159105
00139X

those who rated themselves lower. A high antibody response is a sign of a healthier immune system.

Psychoneuroimmunology (PNI)

Psychoneuroimmunology (PNI) is the study of the relationship between subjective moods and the body's nervous and immune systems. In the past most of the PNI studies focused on the relationship between negative emotions and poor health.

The focus of PNI studies has been the examination of individual immune-cell types, or molecular messengers such as cortisol, or individual genes. The mapping of the human genome in 2003 has enabled researchers to look at the immune system as a whole.

A study[50] in 2007 looked at the gene expression in the white blood cells of six chronically lonely people. These were people who felt lonely or isolated, and were fearful of other people and had felt so for a number of years. The lonely people were contrasted with eight people who claimed to have great friends and social support. The study

---

[50]

http://genomebiology.biomedcentral.com/articles/10.1186/gb-2007-8-9-r189

identified 209 genes out of approximately 22,000 genes in the human genome, that the researchers claimed distinguished the lonely people from the sociable ones. The genes in question either produced more or less of an individual protein. This pattern was consistent across both groups.

Although the study was small it was one of the first to link a psychological risk factor with a broad underlying change in gene expression.

The results were replicated in a slightly larger study[51] of 93 people. A study[52] published in 2013 looked at gene expression and happiness. 80 subjects were asked 14 questions, regarding how happy they felt. Questions such as how often in the past week they had felt happy or satisfied, and how often they felt that their life had a sense of meaning. The researchers identified two forms of happiness:

> *Hedonic* well-being which is characterized by material or bodily pleasures such as eating well or having sex.

---

[51] http://www.pnas.org/content/108/7/3080

[52] http://www.pnas.org/content/110/33/13684

> *Eudaimonic* well-being which is characterised by deeper satisfaction from activities with a greater meaning or purpose, such as intellectual pursuits, social relationships or charity work.

They found that individuals who expressed the Eudaimonic form of well-being had favourable gene-expression profiles. Those who expressed the Hedonic form of well-being had profiles similar to those seen in individuals facing adversity. The researchers believe that the reason for the difference is stress. Hedonic well being is more stressful because it is driven by consumption and the individual's personal circumstances. Eudaimonic well being is less stressful because of its focus on things beyond themselves such as community, politics and art.

These conclusions, and PNI research in general have attracted some criticism. James Coyne, a health psychologist and emeritus professor at the University of Pennsylvania in Philadelphia, claims that the well-being study is simply too small to show anything useful.

Is There a Happiness Gene?

A recent study[53] by Jan-Emmanuel De Neve of University College London identified a possible candidate for a 'happiness gene'. The gene in question 5-HTTLPR [54] is involved in the transport of serotonin. The neurotransmitter serotonin is associated with the reducing of the levels of stress hormones in the body. Genetic variations in 5-HTTLPR appear to be linked to various mood disorders, such as depression. For this reason 5-HTTLPR has also been labelled the 'depression gene'. De Neve studied twins, using the National Longitudinal Study of Adolescent Health (ADD Health)[55] and the Framingham Heart Study[56]. The ADD Health study is a long term study of 20,000 adolescents in the USA, using interviews and questionnaires. Part of the study looks at twins who have grown up together. Data from the twins is used in examining the effects of genetic factors on behaviour. Subjects in De Neve's study were questioned about their moods and life satisfaction to try to determine the effects of heredity and

---

[53]

https://papers.ssrn.com/sol3/papers.cfm?abstract_id=1553633

[54] https://en.wikipedia.org/wiki/5-HTTLPR

[55] http://www.cpc.unc.edu/projects/addhealth

[56] https://www.framinghamheartstudy.org/

environment. De Neve compared the responses of fraternal twins who share 50% of their genes with identical twins who share 100% of their genes. He found a higher correlation between life satisfaction and 5-HTLLPR gene length for identical twins than fraternal twins. De Neve concluded that genetics play an important role in happiness. People who have short 5-HTLLPR genes appear to be more vulnerable to depression and coping with stress. Genetic variation may account for as much as 35% [57] of the overall variation in life satisfaction and happiness. De Neve points out that despite these results it is unlikely that there is one single 'happiness gene'. Our happiness is probably determined by a huge number of genes as well as by environmental elements.

---

[57] Genetics of wellbeing and its components satisfaction with life, happiness, and quality of life: a review and meta-analysis of heritability studies.

Toxic Stress

Numerous studies have found a link between negative emotions and poor health. Heart disease, stroke, and diabetes have all been linked to serious stress over a sustained period. Julius B. Richmond FAMRI Professor of Child Health and Development at HSPH and at the Harvard Graduate School of Education, and Professor of Pediatrics at Harvard Medical School refers to a condition called:

'Toxic Stress'[58]. is defined as frequent of prolonged exposure to physical or emotional abuse in childhood such as chronic neglect, caregiver substance abuse or mental illness, exposure to violence, without adequate adult support. Prolonged activation of the stress response systems can have detrimental effects on the development of the brain and other organs, increasing the risk for stress-related disease in later years.

In conclusion, happiness has many benefits as well as making you generally feel better. All of these benefits can be achieved by your own actions. Your

---

[58]

http://pediatrics.aappublications.org/content/early/2011/12/21/p
eds.2011-2663

individual happiness is largely under your own control. I say *largely* under your control, because it is not completely under your control. There is a social aspect to happiness that we will explore in the next chapter.

.

7

HAPPINESS AT WORK

In this chapter we will focus on happiness from a social perspective. Individual happiness is only part of the equation. To be truly happy you need other people to be happy too.

So far we have focused on ways in which you can make yourself happy. What about other people? As Aristotle once said[59] "man is by nature a social animal." As such we are affected by other people, by their attitudes, moods and behaviour.

One of the great benefits of happiness is that it is 'infectious', you generally feel happier when you encounter someone who is happy. The SMILE approach, inherently affects other people in a

---

[59] Aristole Politics, Book 1

positive way. Simply by looking for the best in others and trying to stop moaning and control your own worrying you will have a positive effect upon other people's levels of happiness.

The social aspect of happiness means more than making the people around you happy, it means living in a happy society. Governments certainly think so; they try to measure the happiness of their people.

Personal Well-being in the UK

Since 2012 the Government in the UK have been attempting to measure the happiness of the nation. The Office for National Statistics asks four questions as part of the Annual Population Survey. Respondents are asked 'how satisfied are you with your life?' 'To what extent do you feel the things you do in your life are worthwhile?' 'How happy did you feel yesterday?' and 'How anxious did you feel yesterday?'

People were asked to respond on a scale from 0 to 10. This is what they found[60] regarding personal

---

60

https://www.ons.gov.uk/peoplepopulationandcommunity/wellb
eing/bulletins/measuringnationalwellbeing/2015to2016

well-being in the UK in 2015-2016:

Life satisfaction was 7.7 out of 10

Feeling what you do in life is worthwhile was 7.8 out of 10

Happiness yesterday was 7.5 out of 10

Anxiety yesterday was 2.9 out of 10

The Happiest Place to Live in the UK

In 2007 First Direct Bank produced a "happiness index" poll[61] to find the best place to live in the UK. Bournemouth won with 82% approval. In 2015 Rightmove, an online estate agency in the UK, produced its own[62] "happiness index". They asked people to rate where they live on community, appearance and price. Harrogate came top with Bournemouth not even featuring in the top ten.

---

[61] : http://www.dailymail.co.uk/news/article-441066/That-happiness-index-full.html

[62]http://www.telegraph.co.uk/finance/newsbysector/constructionandproperty/11785492/The-happiness-index-Where-is-the-worst-place-to-live-in-the-UK.html

The Happiest Countries in the World

The Sustainable Development Solutions Network (SDSN) published the first annual World Happiness Report[63] in 2012. Data is collected from over 150 participating countries. Variables such as, GDP per capita, Social support, healthy life expectancy, freedom to make choices, generosity and trust are measured. Each variable is scored on a 0 to 10 measure. In 2016 out of a total of 157 Denmark came first with a score of 7.526. The UK scored 6.725 coming in at 23rd and the USA came in at 13th with a score of 7.04.

Individual Happiness and Society

There is a worldwide interest in promoting happiness both individually and communally. Individual happiness in itself creates a happier society. Society is composed of individuals, the more happy individuals there are, the happier society will be as a whole. That is true, but society is more than a collection of individuals; it is a collection of different institutions each with its own goals and interests. To promote a truly happy

---

[63] https://en.wikipedia.org/wiki/World_Happiness_Report

society it would be necessary not only for the people working in these institutions to be happy but for the institutions themselves to promote happiness in their workforce.

Happiness at Work

The numerous institutions in society might be broadly divided in to two classes, leisure and work. The term 'institution' in this context refers to any stable, valued, recurring pattern of behaviour. Leisure institutions primarily exist for the pleasure of their users such as hobbies, pastimes, and holidays. Examples of leisure institutions would include football teams, cinema going, gardening, tourism, etc. Work here is defined as everything else, so anything that you are not doing primarily for the pleasure of doing it, is work. Factories and offices fall into this category as do charity work, campaign groups, government etc. You don't have to be paid for some activity in order for it to be considered work. Work can and should be pleasurable; it is nevertheless defined as work because pleasure is not the primary aim.

If the aim is to promote a happier society then it is important to promote happiness at work. You spend most of your time at work, so if you want to lead a happy life it is important to be happy at work. In order to be happy at work and for businesses to promote happiness in their workforce it is vital to demonstrate that happiness at work supports the other goals of the business such as productivity and efficiency.

Happiness and Productivity

A recent study[64] at the University of Warwick found that happiness made people around 12% more productive. Four different experiments were conducted using over 700 participants. In the first experiment a comedy movie clip was played to a group of subjects and their performance measured doing some standardised tasks. It was found that the group who watched the clip substantially outperformed a control group who didn't see the clip.

In the second experiment the first experiment was repeated over a period of time to measure the sustainability of the increased performance over

---

64

http://www2.warwick.ac.uk/fac/soc/economics/staff/academic/proto/workingpapers/happinessproductivity.pdf time. They found the greatest productivity boost in subjects who experienced the greatest improvement in happiness.

The third experiment involved providing chocolate fruit and drinks instead of movie clips, in an attempt to emulate the types of policy an employer might use to promote happiness in the workforce. Once again they found that the increase in productivity was substantial.

The fourth experiment tried to examine how lower happiness in the form of real world events, such as bereavement and family illness might affect productivity. Each subject's productivity was measured and they were then asked to complete questionnaires regarding recent family tragedies. They found that those who reported tragedies showed significantly lower productivity.

A paper[65] published in 2010 examined the question of "Happiness at Work". They found that the 'happy worker is a productive worker hypothesis' may be even truer than at first thought. Individuals at work

---

65

http://epublications.bond.edu.au/cgi/viewcontent.cgi?article=13 07&context=business_pubs

were found to be happier than usual when they believed they were performing better than usual. Job satisfaction, engagement, and affective commitment had important consequences for both individuals and organizations. The paper concluded that "Happiness at work is likely to be the glue that retains and motivates the high quality employees of the future."

Happiness and Stress at Work

Although happiness may make employees more productive, most people's jobs are stressful. Work is stressful; with excessively high workloads, unrealistic deadlines, demanding bosses, lack of resources, inadequate training etc. Stress and happiness are incompatible; to be happy at work it would be necessary to create a more relaxed working environment. Lets examine stress at work to try and answer this question.

Stress in the Workplace

The Health and Safety Executive (HSE) is a non-departmental public body responsible for workplace health, safety and welfare in the UK. The HSE reported[66] 488,000 cases of work related stress, depression or anxiety in 2015/16. The total number of working days lost was 11.7 million days. The main work factors causing work related stress, depression or anxiety were workload pressures, including tight deadlines and too much responsibility and a lack of managerial support. In the USA workplace stress is estimated to cost U.S. employers $200 billion per year in absenteeism, lower productivity, staff turnover, workers' compensation, medical insurance and other stress-related expenses.

Types of Stress

Eustress

Not all stress is bad. Eustress is the term used for positive or beneficial stress. Eustress triggers the body's survival mechanism, but in a way that we feel that we are still in control. Examples of eustress include the excitement you feel on a roller-coaster ride, seeing a scary movie, or overcoming a challenge. Eustress can make you feel invigorated it boosts your energy and allows you to perform better.

---

[66] http://www.hse.gov.uk/statistics/causdis/stress/index.htm

Acute Stress

Acute stress triggers the survival mechanism when we feel we are not in control. Imminent danger triggers acute stress. Acute stress is the most common form of stress. Eustress can tip into acute stress.

Chronic Stress

Long term stress is known as chronic stress, when we repeatedly face stressors that we are unable to control. Most of the stress referred to by the HSE and other bodies in their reports is chronic stress.

Causes of Stress at Work

HSE have identified six causes of stress[67] in the workplace:

Unreasonable demands placed upon employees.

A lack of control in the way that employees do their job.

A lack of support or inadequate information

---

[67]

http://www.hse.gov.uk/stress/furtheradvice/causesofstress.htm

and support from their colleagues and superiors.

Poor relationships at work including unacceptable behaviour such as bullying.

Poorly defined role and responsibilities.

Poor communication regarding organisational changes.

HSE stresses the importance of understanding each of the six factors and how they relate to each other, as this can influence the amount of stress an individual experiences:

Giving employees more control over their work can reduce the impact of high demands.

Increasing the levels of support by colleagues and managers will also reduce the impact of high demands.

Stamping out bullying and harassment and replacing a work culture of blame with one of respect will help solve problems with poor relationships at work.

Problems with roles and responsibilities are probably the easiest problems to solve.

Communicating and managing changes effectively at the organisational level as well as changes to individuals or will reduce levels of stress.

Does a Relaxed Working Environment Lower Productivity?

To get the most out of their workforce, employers want to generate a certain amount of stress. Stress in the form of eustress will energise people and help them focus on the tasks in hand. Eustress, will instil a drive for success in employees and help create a sense of responsibility. A certain level of stress will teach people to tolerate more stress.

The problem with creating stress in the workplace is that it can quickly become counterproductive. Eustress becomes acute stress which may turn into chronic stress. Once a stressed workplace culture has been created, individual employees become less productive, they spend more time worrying about social interactions and handling conflicts, and less time collaborating and working effectively.

Targets and deadlines are sometimes manipulated to generate stress. Failure to meet targets and deadlines can result in various levels of blame and public humiliation. Fear that employees will waste time and not work hard enough is one of the reasons that targets and deadlines are manipulated and procedures over regulated. The more rigid the control there is in the workplace, the more likely are employees are to react against it. Relaxed work scheduling can relieve stress and boost productivity. The introduction of flexitime for employees juggling work and family obligations, makes them feel valued, increasing their self esteem, making them happier and more productive. Allowing employees to work at home on a part- or full-time basis or to set their own schedules gives them more control, boosting productivity by reducing stress and helping employees to focus better.

The aim is not to eliminate stress completely, but to control it, and more importantly let the employees control it as far as possible. Obviously some controls and procedures are necessary, for example those designed for safety and hygiene. People tend not to mind controls and procedures as long as they understand the reason for them. Ill defined guidelines, procedures, duties and roles can be as detrimental as overly strict ones. Creating an environment where employees understand what is required and can work in a blame free culture where people can communicate openly is the key to success.

To answer to the question: "Does a relaxed working environment lower productivity?" The answer is No, a relaxed workplace 'is more productive than a stressful one. Professor Oswald, one of the researchers[68] from the University of Warwick, put it very well when he stated "Companies like Google have invested more in employee support and employee satisfaction has risen as a result. For Google, it rose by 37%, they know what they are talking about. Under scientifically controlled conditions, making workers happier really pays off." An effective workplace is relaxed but not relaxing.

---

[68]

http://www2.warwick.ac.uk/fac/soc/economics/staff/academic/proto/workingpapers/happinessproductivity.pdf

The Benefits of a Relaxed Work Environment

The benefits of a more relaxed workplace are threefold; there are economic benefits, benefits to individual employees and management benefits:

Economic Benefits

Improved return on investment in training and development because of lower staff turnover.

Lower risk of expensive litigation because legal obligations have been complied with.

A reduction in the costs of sick pay, sickness cover, overtime and recruitment.

An improvement in customer care and relationships with clients and suppliers.

Benefits for Individual Employees

Being happy at work and not wanting to leave

Feeling more motivated and committed to your work

Higher morale in general

The ability to work harder and perform better with the potential to increase your earning power

Feeling part of a team and the decision-making process, so you are able to better accept changes

Better relationships with your managers and team members.

As a line manager you can demonstrate good management skills that could help your career development.

Management Benefits

Improvements in productivity.

Improvements in work quality.

A reduction in staff turnover and intention to leave, so improving retention.

Better absence management

A reduction in days lost to sickness and absenteeism

Fewer accidents

The Problem with Measuring Happiness

The problem with trying to measure well-being or happiness is that it is a subjective experience. Using a scale from 0 to 10 to measure happiness is fraught with problems. My capacity for, or experience of happiness may be completely different from yours. The feelings of happiness on our personal scales are likely to be wildly different. We are not actually measuring the same thing. Happiness is a qualitative experience and not subject to quantitive analysis. It might be argued that although it is difficult to measure happiness, we are measuring something akin to happiness and we can use whatever it is we have measured to compare how it changes from year to year. We can track our measurement of happiness, however inaccurate it may be, to see if it is increasing or decreasing. The problem here is that, not only are we not sure what we are measuring but we are not sure why it has changed over time. To find out the cause of change we would need to ask a number of supplementary questions. . Let me give you an example. Say we find that people with a University degree score higher in the happiness index we might conclude that education is a key factor in promoting happiness. The problem here is cause and effect, does education make people happier, or do happy people seek out a better education? Or is it a mix of both. Another problem with asking people to report their own happiness, and that it is affected by the way that they feel at the moment that they are reporting it. For example if you are asked to complete a questionnaire about your general level of happiness your emotional state at the time you answer the questions will have a huge effect on your responses. Another factor to be taken into account is the unreliability of people's responses, there is the nostalgia factor or "rose tinted glasses" effect where things always seemed better in the past.

Creating a Happy Work Culture

People Do Not Like Change

Changing the culture of any organisation is not easy. Work cultures have often developed over time. People are resistant to change; they are comfortable with the current culture. Even when the present culture does not best serve the objectives of the business, people still prefer to do it the way it has always been done, regardless of the consequences.

Typically people will only consider cultural change, if they feel they have to. A significant event will occur that forces them to change the way they have been doing things. It might be a significant loss of sales or customers, a new aggressive competitor, or major changes in their industry that gets their attention. The work culture in any organisation reflects the prevailing management style. In smaller organisations that tends to be the style of the founder or owner of the business. In larger organisations the culture is set by the management, who may perpetuate the work culture by recruiting people that have a similar management style to themselves.

Culture is the sum of attitudes, customs and beliefs that distinguish one group of people from another.

A work culture creates a unique brand for a business which helps differentiate it from the competition. For example think of the different cultures in an advertising agency and a solicitor's office, one will want to promote an upbeat, modern, risk taking, culture and the other a traditional, professional, trustworthy culture. The work culture defines the standards and procedures that give the company and employees direction in the way they conduct their daily business.

SMILE at Work

Within any work culture, whatever it is, it is possible to create a happier form of that work culture using the SMILE approach. Use SMILE to enhance the current culture. The four elements of SMILE are not only compatible with every business's objectives but they help promote those objectives. Happy employees are more efficient and productive.

SMILE with its call to 'Stop Moaning', promotes a more pleasant work environment. No one wants to listen to their colleagues complaining all the time. That's not to say that people can't voice legitimate complaints when they are appropriate. 'Stop moaning at work' is all about fostering a positive attitude to your job, your colleagues, your suppliers, and your customers.

'Don't worry about things that you can't do anything about. If you can do something, then do it.' Worries at work tend to be caused by the six stressors identified by the HSE, namely, unreasonable demands, lack of control, lack of support, bullying, poorly defined responsibilities and poor communications. The solution is to do something about it, by giving employees more control, increasing the levels of support, stamping out bullying and clearly define roles and responsibilities.

When you are unable to affect the cause of your worries, then they have to be managed. The open happy, blame free culture that SMILE fosters will encourage employees to talk to their supervisors to try to alleviate their worries. The 'L' SMILE in stands for learning new skills, essential in creating a highly skilled, well-motivated, workforce, capable of producing quality work.

Finally, the SMILE approach advocates empathy when asking you to 'Try to look for the good in people'. Looking for the good in others creates a positive, blame free, open culture. Such a culture enables people to speak openly to their supervisors about their worries and concerns, it reduces the need to complain or moan. People feel free to discuss their own personal work objectives and to ask their supervisors to help plan their next move.

Looking for the best in others boosts morale resulting in lower rates of absenteeism.

Subjective Well-being

The problems associated with trying to measure happiness has led to the introduction of the term "Subjective Well-Being" rather than "happiness." The term "happiness" is thought to be to imprecise. Subjective Well-Being encompasses ideas of satisfaction with life or feelings of fulfillment and ongoing emotional feelings such as joy. The focus of Subjective Well-Being is the subjective element; the individual's own assessment of their feelings rather than some external measure. Subjective Well-Being like "happiness" is an umbrella term. Both terms include several different components, which are independent. It is possible to be generally happy with your life, or subjectively feel that your life is fulfilled at the same time as you experience a negative emotion. Another example of the contradictory nature of the elements of both terms is where you are forced to perform a boring necessary task which makes you unhappy, but you do so because it will lead to your long term happiness. We began this chapter by talking about the dual nature of happiness: happiness as a subjective emotional state and a general state of well-being. Subjective Well-Being is an attempt to bring some precision to the measurement of happiness. Subjective Well-Being like the term "happiness" suffers from the same problems inherent in the dual nature of both definitions. The focus of the SMILE approach is on developing and sustaining happiness over the long term, in creating a happier life. SMILE focuses on the second element of "happiness" or "subjective well-being" that is a general state of well-being. SMILE will bring you many moments of joy and pleasure, but they are not the central aim. Moments of positive emotion are the building blocks on which long term emotional happiness is built, not an end in them selves. Just as leading a happy life may mean that you also lead a morally good life; ethical behaviour is not the central objective of SMILE, it is a positive side effect.

SMILE: A Common Frame of Reference

The mnemonic acronym SMILE is not just a convenient way of reminding yourself of the four injunctions you should use to make yourself happy. SMILE can be used as a common point of reference in any social situation where people have adopted the method. For example at work, if you hear someone moaning about nothing, you could remind them that they are not following the SMILE method, or you might just say that "they are not smiling." The context would remind them that this means stop moaning.

Reminding people that they aren't smiling is a more pleasant and friendlier way of reminding them of what they need to do to be happy than telling them to stop moaning. Telling someone that they have 'stopped smiling' or 'don't forget to smile' is a gentle way of reminding yourself and others to change your behaviour in certain situations.

Changing Your Business Culture

A change in business culture means changing people's behaviour and attitudes. To be successful the new cultural values should permeate through every aspect of the business. Given that people are resistant to change this can not only be very difficult to achieve, but it is a process that will take time. Your existing work culture has developed over many years, so it will take time for the new work culture to become fully established. Every work culture reflects the prevailing management style. Established work cultures reflect the values of the formal leaders, and the 'buy in' of informal leaders. A successful strategy needs to address both formal and informal leaders.

Formal Strategy

Set the mission. Most businesses have a mission statement. You need to formally amend your mission statement to reflect the new cultural values you wish to communicate. I say amend the mission statement, not replace it. Your business still has the same objectives; it is the way in which you seek to achieve those objectives that has changed. You will be looking to achieve a happier workforce, or making X a better place to work etc. Don't be shamefaced about it, be proud that this is one of your core values.

Communication. Success in implementing change comes from effective communication. Your message needs to be communicated to your staff consistently. Typically senior managers communicate the new mission to their key managers who are then expected communicate the message downstream. This is done with varying degrees of emphasis and enthusiasm. To be successful it is vital that every employee hears the mission and embraces it. If change is to be effective it has to be communicated to everyone by the person at the top. There is no employee whose job is so small or insignificant that he or she shouldn't hear this message from the person who took the decision to implement it in person.

Align goals. Set departmental goals that reflect the changes in the mission statement. Ensure that departmental goals are compatible don't set them in isolation.

Training. Train key influencers and areas of the business where change will have the largest impact first. Look for quick wins to demonstrate the effectiveness of the changes.

Share the benefits. Aligning your company around a happy work culture has its benefits. A happy workforce is more productive, and the work is of a higher quality. Staff will embrace the new culture if they can see that it is working for them. Let them share in the material rewards of the new culture.

Informal Strategy

The essence of the informal strategy to change is to use an emotional approach to influence behaviour. The informal strategy should support the formal strategy. Research shows that using an informal emotional approach to change behaviour significantly effects change that will last. According to a survey[69] on culture and change management conducted by the Katzenbach Center only about half of transformation initiatives accomplish and sustain their goals. The reasons cited include "change fatigue", where too many changes are implemented at once. 65% of recipients to the survey claimed to be suffering from "change fatigue". Only around half of the respondents felt their organisation had the capabilities to deliver change. A successful informal strategy should focus on the following:

> *Evolution not revolution.* Don't try to replace your existing work culture entirely; the new values should be compatible with your existing culture. The new culture should be a development of the existing culture, not a wholesale upgrade. Implementing the SMILE

---

[69] http://www.strategyand.pwc.com/reports/cultures-role-organizational-change

approach in a Solicitor's office will be entirely different from implementing it in an advertising agency. Both will be looking to achieve a positive happy workforce, but the outward expression of happiness, will be different in each.

A change in behaviour will cause a change in attitude. It is generally accepted that a change in behaviour requires a change in the way people think[70]. Businesses spend a lot of time trying to convince their staff to change their minds about something, to encourage them to change their behaviour. However,Cognitive dissonance[71] theory as stated by Leo Festinger[72] states that an individual who experiences inconsistency tends to become psychologically uncomfortable. The discomfort associated by behaviour that is inconsistent with your attitudes motivates you try to reduce this dissonance. One of the ways that people tend to reduce dissonance is either to change their behaviour or change their attitudes. Festinger

---

70

https://siteresources.worldbank.org/EXTGOVACC/Resources/BehaviorChangeweb.pdf

[71] https://en.wikipedia.org/wiki/Cognitive_dissonance

[72] https://en.wikipedia.org/wiki/Leon_Festinger

conducted an experiment[73] in 1959 to test this theory. Subjects were divided into two groups. Subjects in each group were tested individually. They were asked to perform an hour of boring and monotonous tasks. One group of subjects were told that the experiment had finished and left, the rest of the subjects were asked by the experimenter to do them a favour. The favour consisted of telling the next participant, who was actually a confederate, that the task was extremely enjoyable. The subjects who did the favour experienced dissonance as the task was in fact extremely boring. Half of the subjects who performed the favour were paid $1 while the other half received $20. When asked about the task afterwards, those who were paid $1 reported the task to be more enjoyable than those who were paid $20. Festinger claimed that those paid $1 were forced to reduce dissonance by changing their opinions about the task. To produce consonance with their behaviour, they decided that the task was more enjoyable than it was. The subjects who were paid $20 for the favour experienced less dissonance, since the large payment provided consonance with their behaviour; as a result they rated the task as less enjoyable. The ratings of the better paid group were in fact similar

---

73

https://faculty.washington.edu/jdb/345/345%20Articles/Festing er%20&%20Carlsmith.pdf

to those who were not asked to perform the dissonance inducing favour. If changing people's behaviour can change their attitudes, then the aim should be to change the way people behave. Changes in behaviour are easier to monitor than changes in attitude. Changes in behaviour should be tangible, actionable, repeatable, observable, and measurable. An example of changes in behaviour designed to promote happiness might focus on increasing levels employee's control. Examples of Individual employee empowerment might range from reducing the number of approvals needed for decisions, to enabling employees to determine their own work processes.

> *Focus on the most important behaviours.* Businesses should be wary of trying to change too much at once. There is a temptation to adopt the 'new broom approach' to minimise the disruption caused by change to get it all over at once. That is a mistake. It is important to identify a few critical behaviours and focus on them. Critical behaviours are those that will have great impact if put into practice by a significant number of people. Ensure that these few critical behaviours are aligned with the business's mission and individual objectives. Reduce the critical behaviours into simple, practical steps that people can take every day. Do not try to implement these new behaviours

throughout the business but select a few groups of employees who have been trained in these behaviours, to champion them. Selected groups should be those that respond strongly to the new behaviours and who are likely to implement and spread them. The SMILE methodology should be implemented among a few influential groups to create broad acceptance within the organisation.

Use the influence of informal leaders. Informal leaders in any organisation are those whom others follow. They do not need to be in positions of authority. Jon Katzenbach, founder of the Katzenbach Center, a global institute on organizational culture and leadership, identifies four types of informal leader:[74] "Pride builders" who are able to motivate other people, and are often catalysts for improvement around them. "Exemplars" who act as role models. Exemplars tend to be well respected and are effective peer influencers. "Networkers" are the informal communicators within an organisation. Networkers know lots of people, and communicate freely and openly with them." Early adopters" like to be first with anything new; they enjoy experimenting with new

---

[74] http://www.forbes.com/sites/strategyand/2016/02/28/four-types-of-authentic-informal-leaders/#1fd30332353a

technologies, processes, and ways of working. Informal leaders can quickly spread positive as well as negative attitudes to cultural change, so ensure that you win them over. Informal leaders will quickly propagate your messages throughout the organisation both face to face and via social media.

Ensure that change is supported throughout the organisation. It is tempting to see anything to do with changing roles and responsibilities as solely the responsibility of Human Resources. To be successful change needs to be fully supported by managers in every part of the company. The important new behaviours need to be exhibited by the formal as well as the informal leaders. Emotional commitment to change among influencers should be visible in order to set the tone for others to follow. If an organisation is espousing one type of behaviour and staff, see management behaving inconsistently they will ignore the type of behaviour the organisation is espousing and simply copy their managers.

Key behaviours should be linked to business objectives. Discussions about cultural change often focus on abstract concepts such as values, feelings and motivations. These are important but employees also need to understand the impact that these abstract concepts will have on them. Senior Managers often address their staff and talk in general terms about the need to change, and simply leave employees confused. When discussing change it is important to provide tangible, well-defined examples of the new behaviours and explain why they are important in terms of tangible benefits.

Look for quick wins. If people are to embrace cultural change they need to see the benefits and see them quickly. If people don't see positive results of the change in the short term they will grow cynical. It is extremely important to demonstrate the impact of cultural change on business results as quickly as possible. Choose areas of the business where you can demonstrate a quick win to implement the changes first.

Look for potential conflicts. Quickly identify any potential conflicts in the way that you have always done business and the new behaviours you are seeking to introduce. Make sure that you resolve these potential conflicts by aligning the two. You should also make sure that there is no possible conflict in the messages that the informal leaders are sharing and the messages that management are promoting. Make sure that all your mechanisms for promoting cultural change are aligned.

Take a long term view. Change is a slow process, it has to be fostered and managed over time. It is very easy for the old culture to resurrect itself once the novelty of the new has worn off. To be successful you should actively monitor, manage, care for, and update your forces of cultural change.

In Conclusion

The conclusion of the book is the beginning of the adventure, where you start to put SMILE into practice in your everyday life. Follow the rules and adapt them to your own situation.

I have deliberately arranged the book into sections so you can also use it as a quick reference guide. I have included tips and advice throughout the book to help you follow the rules.

I don't pretend that the advice and tips I have given are exhaustive. I'm sure that as you start to put the rules into practice in your own life you will find new strategies for new situations as they arise.

Please visit my website where you can share your own experiences with me and other readers. Let's share our success stories and learn from each other's mistakes.

http://www.makinghappinessahabit.com

Happiness, like life itself is not an end but a process.
Constant repetition and adaptation of SMILE will
transform your personality to make happiness your
default state. Remember if your face won't SMILE
make it.

INDEX

A

B

C

JEREMY KITT

Jeremy Kitt is a motivational speaker and business trainer. He has over twenty years experience as a manager in Global Telecommunications with Siemens and Ericsson. Jeremy runs his own successful web design business in Kent.

21596355R00115

Printed in Great Britain
by Amazon